Battle Hymn

of the

Tiger Daughter

How one family fought the myth that
you need to destroy childhood
in order to raise extraordinary adults.

DIANA AND HANA HOLQUIST

Excerpt

...People wonder how American parents raise such innovative, creative, kick-butt children. What is it that these parents do to create kids with the courage to follow their dreams? Kids who defy the word "stereotype"? Kids capable of seeing beyond the outdated, conventional (yawn!) clichés—Harvard, violin, doctor, lawyer—and into a future that most parents are too old, tradition-bound, and small-minded to even imagine? Well, I can tell you, because I know. Here are a few things that my children, Hana and Isaiah, are never allowed to do:

- *Miss an episode of* The Office.
- *Waste their time on extracurricular activities that they don't love.*
- *Pass up important family or social events because they put their own personal enrichment first.*
- *Think that they're better than other kids because of their grades. An "A" can mean excellent, but it can also stand for "asshole."*
- *Brag about awards. The only achievements that matter in the end don't get awards (character, kindness, compassion, courage, friendship).*

I'm using the term "American parents" loosely. Anyone who embraces the Western values of individuality, creativity, and questioning of authority can be American in my book. But let's face it, most people with these values live in the West. Specifically, in America.

Quite a few of them live in my house...

PART I:
Meeting Hana

"Your time is limited. Don't waste it living someone else's life."

--Steve Jobs

Chapter 1

by Diana: A Tiger in the House

My friend lent me a book called *Battle Hymn of the Tiger Mother*. It was the memoir of self-described "Chinese mother," Amy Chua. Chua touted her brand of extreme parenting in the name of cultural supremacy: no play dates, no sleepovers, no grade below an A, must be two years ahead of peers in math, must play either the piano or violin, and so on.

"Don't buy the book," my friend told me. "I don't want this insane nightmare of a mother to make any more money."

I couldn't wait to read this. I love people who get other people riled up, and Tiger Mother was a doozy.

The book described episodes of screaming, ranting, and otherwise belittling her young children. Tiger Mother called her daughters fat and lazy. She forced them to practice their chosen instruments (chosen from either the violin or the piano) for hours every day, even on family vacations. "The first hour is the easy one," she wrote.

That's how it is in our house, too, only with marathon sessions on the couch, watching *The Office*.

I was simultaneously horrified and intrigued. Were my kids lazy? Fat? Doomed? Hana is fourteen; Isaiah is twelve. I let them play video games. I let them watch television. I let them eat sugary snacks. Heck, I let them eat sugary breakfasts. They have Facebook profiles and spend hours on-line "chatting" with their friends and texting on their cell phones. I let them have sleepovers and play dates. I let them be in school plays. I let them spend summers lolling around the house, doing God-knows-what while I shut myself in my study upstairs to work on my novels.

I, more or less, let them be.

Was my lax attitude contributing to the decline of America? Of the entire Western world?

Don't laugh; I took these questions seriously. I felt a responsibility to society at large. What could my video-playing, reality-show-crazed, sugar-hyped children contribute to our family, our country, our culture? Did Tiger Mother have it right? Was she seeing the bigger picture that I was too complacent and lazy to notice?

Stop.

Wait.

Hold the heck on.

We were laid back, but we weren't exactly slackers.

My husband is a tenured professor at an Ivy League university.

I graduated from an Ivy League school (Columbia, class of 1989), was a copywriter in some of New York City's best ad agencies, and am now a successful novelist.

But it's my kids who are truly awesome.

Isaiah is a straight-A student. Naturally, he's in advanced math. He's also a star athlete, training with a select group of twelve year olds in the Philadelphia Union developmental program. Yes, *that* Union—Philadelphia's professional Major League soccer team. In his spare time, as if there is such a thing when you train six days a week at the highest level and go to school full time, he plays cello and maintains an active social life.

Hana is also a straight-A student. Her passions are knitting, sewing, crafting, embroidering, beading, painting, and drawing. She spends her Saturdays at a prestigious art college in downtown Philadelphia taking classes that she pays for with scholarships from her art teachers. She also plays the viola. Last year she was asked to join the chamber orchestra, an honor she turned down as she was too busy with other all-consuming interests (at the moment, costume design and boxing).

Did I mention that Hana has her own business, Hanacorn, which makes custom hoodies and other hand-crafted fashion accessories?

Yes, yes she does.

So what exactly was going on here? How had we achieved upper-middle-class, high-achieving nirvana without the stress, anxiety, shouting, or emotional violence that tiger parenting endorses?

Or—Oh my God!—maybe we hadn't achieved anything. Maybe our easy-going, above-average complacency masked a tragic flaw: we weren't successful enough.

Enough for what? What exactly was Tiger Mother after? Status? Riches? Fame? Or should I take her at her word that all she wanted was to raise tough, resilient children who weren't spoiled and coddled like my Western children? Because Lord knows, my kids worked like dogs in a frightening and unjust world; I loved to coddle.

I started to read sections of *Tiger Mother* out loud to my kids. We tackled the final uncomfortable chapters over breakfast one weekend morning wherein the younger "rebel" tiger cub quits all-consuming violin to take up ubercompetitive tennis that her mother micromanages secretly via text messages to the coach.

"So," I asked my kids. "Do you wish I was tougher with you guys?"

"Yes!" They both cried.

It took a while to untangle that they each thought I wasn't tough enough on their sibling. Hana thought I babied Isaiah. Isaiah thought Hana got away with murder. (See, coddling, above.)

"But what about you? Do you wish I was tougher on you?"

"You can't be a tiger mother," Hana said.

"Why not?"

"Because in this house," she said, "I'm the tiger."

"What's that make me?" I asked.

"Prey." She said it with a devious smile.

"*Off-key Ditty of the Sloth Mother*," Isaiah suggested.

My children were not displaying the Eastern ideal of respect for their elders. For this, I was delighted. I loved their rebellion, their fearless, spontaneous wordplay, and their open opposition. This was the stuff of Western creativity and ingenuity. Our great country was built on rebellion, not slavish kowtowing to an unjust, unyielding emperor.

Go USA!

"*Battle Hymn of the Bald Eagle Mother*," I suggested.

"That sounds awful," Hana pointed out. "No one wants advice

from endangered birds."

While they got into an argument over whether the bald eagle was still endangered, I contemplated the heart of the issue: what was my battle hymn? Did I even have one? You can say a lot of things about tiger mothers, but at least they know where they stand.

Did I? Or was I just bumbling through and had gotten lucky with two awesome kids?

Hell, no. I knew exactly why my kids were outstanding. I'd just never thought much about it. It seemed so obvious, it didn't warrant discussion. But after reading tiger mother's self-satisfied ranting, I realized that two purely Western values set my children—and all children raised the "Western" way—on the path to true success. That is, the path to personal achievement, material comfort, and mental health.

First, Western culture recognizes and celebrates the importance of an inner life. Feelings matter; individual desires matter. Therefore, controlling, exploitive, intolerant, and violent behavior toward the powerless is frowned upon. This is why what tiger mothers call discipline, Western mothers recognize as potentially harmful neurosis. China is one of the most mentally ill countries in the world, with one in five adults suffering from a mental illness. Suicide is the leading cause of death among young people[1]. If this is the culture at the root of tiger parenting, no thanks.

The second reason my kids are awesome is that I don't give a crap about achievement. That dull list of exploits I rattled off a few pages back—who cares? Those accomplishments are the least interesting aspects about any of us. Judging children (or adults) by their "elite" awards and honors strikes introspective, deep-thinking Westerners as pathetic insecurity. Pathetic insecurity is the territory of a culture that values what other people think above all else, a culture in which fitting in is paramount. That isn't my culture. I live in a society that praises the rebel, the dreamer, and the outcast. Only with this attitude firmly in hand can children break the mold, believe in themselves, and achieve truly great things.

But I hadn't always been quite so clear thinking. I understood the appeal of tiger mothers and the multi-million dollar industry that

---

[1] The New Yorker Magazine, January 10th, 2011 "Meet Dr. Freud: Does psychoanalysis have a future in an authoritarian state?" Even Osnos.

catered to them because I'd been there and done that. "You know," I told my kids. "It might surprise you guys, but I used to a tiger mother."

"No way." They looked shocked, as if I'd just announced that I used to be a pole dancer.

"It's a long story. But I'm reformed. I totally accept the errors of my ways."

"You should write a book," Hana said. "Put out another point of view. I know kids who have tiger mothers, and some of them really need help."

"Exactly. That's why it's a story you guys should tell, not me," I said.

They didn't look game.

"We should write it together. Alternating chapters," I tried.

Isaiah caught the gleam in my eye and ducked out the back door, cell phone in hand, texting wildly. He and I were already writing a book together about the insanity of super-elite youth soccer. He knew how time consuming and annoying I could be when I was on a joint writing project.

Hana watched her brother jump on his bike and disappear down the driveway. He shot her an ironic salute through the window. "Uh oh," she said.

"I'll do the typing," I assured her. "I'll interview you. It'll be fun."

She crossed her arms over her chest, but I could tell she was intrigued. That tiger mother book had really gotten her goat. "*Battle Hymn of the Tiger Daughter*," she said.

From the mouth of babes.

I pushed aside the breakfast mess and opened my MacBook. "Tell me about those kids you know."

She smiled.

And I did what Tiger Mother never even considered: I shut up and let my daughter have the floor.

Chapter 2

by Hana: Be the Tiger

I will eat you alive.

I roar sometimes. Also growl. A lot. That's okay, since I'm a teenager. It's what I'm supposed to do. If you're a growling grown up, please stop. That's ridiculous. It's my time now.

If you want to know what makes me so ferocious, that's what this book is about. If you're an adult, what makes me dangerous is you. You are trying to control me. But I will not be controlled.

I don't go in for that dancing monkey stuff.

What's dancing monkey stuff?

I perform; you clap.

THIS IS NOT WHAT MY LIFE IS ABOUT.

Don't get me wrong. Playing instruments or running around after soccer balls or dancing till your blisters get blisters so your parents can watch and clap and brag to all their friends is fine if that's what you want to do.

But is it really what you want to do?

Know who you are, what you love, and then love that thing with a passion and don't let anyone stop you. You can't possibly figure out your passion if you're playing an instrument three hours a day since you were a baby.

Do you love the playing or the clapping? Are you your parents' little puppet? Their mini-me? If they're clapping for you, you might want to think twice about whom you're trying to please. If they're horrified and confused by you, well, you might be on to something good.

Dear Tiger Children: Tell your parents to shut the fruitcake up. Say it nicely, if you want, but say it. Because your life is all you have—and it's not theirs.

In fact, they can ruin it for you if you let them. Believe me, I see it happen all around me all the time to some of my good friends.

They do what their parents say until they have no idea what they want anymore.

But guess what? Your parents will get old and die.

And then what?

So get on it, girl (or boy). What do you love?

You are the tiger.

Roar.

Before it's too late.

Chapter 3

by Diana: How I Lost My Mojo

I never cared what anyone thought of me. I achieved, but only with a sly nod to the stupidity of the need to prove myself to the bunch of old fogies who controlled the world (but not for much longer). Hard work led to good grades, led to good college, led to good job. It was a game I played, but I recognized it as a game. I never valued it. I thought that people who were impressed that I went to Columbia University were chumps who bought the hype. Columbia was great, of course. But not everyone there was impressive, not even most of the kids. Some, of course, were extraordinary. But some were average. Some were legacies, the sons or daughters of alumni. Some were good at chasing a tennis ball or came from Alaska where the competition to get in wasn't nearly as fierce. In other words, they were a fair representation of the people I'd always known growing up in my wealthy suburb. Why anyone would believe that these kids were special because they were rich, connected, and compliant enough to push all the right buttons was beyond me.

By the time I graduated Columbia, I wanted out. It was one thing to toe the line for adults while I was a child in order to do what I wanted on the side (hang out with boys and friends). This felt like a perfectly natural form of self-preservation. But now that I was officially an independent adult, I could fend for myself and stop abusing the approval of those who funded me.

But what to do?

I wanted to do the opposite of my status-obsessed, conventional, frightened classmates who followed all the rules in exchange for advancement, status, and profit. My peers were becoming doctors or lawyers or going on to graduate degrees, most of them for lack of anything better to do. Don't misunderstand—I had some classmates with passions who went on to achieve great things. But they were few and far between, as is the case in the world in general. Also, I have nothing against doctors or lawyers—if they're passionate. But most of the kids I knew were lost and confused about what to do now that their carefully prescribed path had ended. They stood at the edge of the dark woods of opportunity, peered in, then scampered off to find another path that traced a cautious, wide circle around the dangerous unknown.

I wanted to do something different. Something fun. Something far outside my comfort zone. So I plunged into the creative department of a New York advertising agency with abandon. I loved that most of my new colleagues hadn't gone to good schools if they'd even gone to school at all. By the time I was twenty-five, I had clawed and slaved to New York's most coveted junior-level ad job-a copywriter on the Pepsi account.

Be young. Have fun. Drink Pepsi.

Right on.

Many of my coworkers were drinkers—and not of Pepsi. Many were recreational drug users. All were artists, writers, and musicians.

These people were brilliant. Their brilliance was amplified because they thumbed their noses at conservative America, which didn't welcome people like these people. Thirty years after the age of *Mad Men*, the creative department of ad agencies was still packed with Jews, Italians, queers, and worst of all, artists. The account services people were still mostly WASPs and Ivy League strivers. At any decent agency, the creative department ruled.

One day we got a hold of a questionnaire one of the senior account people had filled out that seemed to confirm our view of the world. It was from the publishing company that put out *The Seven Habits of Highly Effective People* book series. We guffawed at the executive's self-serving answers on why she was such a success: be up by five in the morning, work on weekends, never give up.

Yeah, right.

We knew the truth of this sort of corporate success. This lady was a moron. She was the wife of a company muckety-muck. We could tell you her seven secrets without any questionnaire: be born into money, marry into more money (preferably, a powerful account exec), be white, be blonde, do as you're told, don't stir the pot, and kiss ass—lots of it.

But my colleagues weren't bitter. They had no pretensions, no desire to play it straight. They didn't have mothers who had held their hands and told them what to do or families who had paid their way. They were hustlers who worked like dogs. Eighty hour work weeks were nothing. We ate and slept at the office. When Super Bowl ad time came, we didn't eat or sleep at all. Advertising was brutally competitive. People weren't nice.

"Come back when it's funny," my creative director would say.

I loved that guy.

Then my husband got his first academic job as a Russian history professor at Cornell University and we moved to Ithaca, New York. I should mention that my husband was no rule-following, pretentious conformist either. He dropped out of high school from boredom and went to his local state university because it was there and it was cheap. Luckily, it was also excellent. Indiana University gave him everything he needed to succeed, including a life-long love of state schools and a mistrust of the blind worship of the Ivies. His love of history was scary-intense, as anyone who knows him can attest. But it was pure. He was never forced to do anything by anyone and he never paid a dime for any of his advanced degrees. He was the consummate academic, destined to it, with no greater love. He was, in a word, an intellectual.

Since his career was so specialized, we had agreed when we married that we would go where his career called. No worries. I'd seen what happened to my ancient (over thirty) colleagues. Their home lives were hell because of the hours and travel. *Be old. Have an unhappy, neglected spouse and kids. Drink scotch.*

Part of thumbing my nose at the conventional world was being able to change my life on a dime without fear of the future.

Luckily, Ithaca New York was not part of the conventional world. Ithaca, as the locals liked to say, was centrally isolated. It was hippie, progressive heaven, studded with natural wonders and home to a cult-run Mate Yerba shop on the main drag. It was voted the number one town for lesbians in the United States by *The Utne Reader*. And yes, the general population actually read *The Utne Reader*. Ithaca was cold. It was gray. It was not an advertising mecca. In fact, there were pretty much no jobs at all for people like me. We were aptly called *trailing spouses*.

So I had a child. A beautiful baby girl.

And then, just like that, something strange happened to me. Although, as I learned later, perhaps it wasn't quite so strange, as it seemed to happen to a lot of parents.

I lost my mind.

Hana was perfect. Blonde hair, blue eyes, charming smile. I had never been up close and personal with a creature so absolutely pure. Anything was possible for this amazing child. She stirred a primal feeling inside me: pride.

Pride was, of course, the original and most serious of the deadly sins. I wasn't religious and didn't believe in sin. But I had seen with my own eyes the unholy presence of assholes on this earth, those proud people who walked among us, noses in the air. They were absurd. The worst of them, the raging narcissists ("raging narcissist" is Western-speak for "tiger mother") were absurd and cruel. Yet, when I went to my vegan pot-luck baby group every Thursday afternoon and our tiny babies lay on their backs and cooed, I watched the other babies with narrowed eyes.

Hana cooed the best.

What was this competitive nonsense that had begun to keep me up at night? Was it born of fear? Fear of what, exactly? Or maybe it wasn't fear, but hope. Hana's huge eyes were pools in which I saw my own reflection, and I fell madly in love. My sense of pride in my daughter (in myself?) felt good. I got a visceral rush out of her insane beauty and obvious genius as if it were a drug. The boundaries between us were delightfully blurred. Getting a rush out of my own looks and accomplishments took incredibly hard work; the possibility for failure was immense. But this itty-bitty baby rush came easy. I didn't have to do a thing, because she did it all just by existing.

Until, of course, like any high, I needed more. I became accustomed to the beauty and brilliance of my infant daughter. Add to that the disturbing downer of other children who were also so beautiful, so brilliant. They were such a buzz kill for a mother like me who was sure her daughter was the second coming, not of Christ (I'm Jewish) but more mesmerizingly of *me*! But a better me. A me done right, my way.

The power was as intoxicating as the pride.

There was just one way to up my dose: I had to prove that my child was beautiful and brilliant so that others could shower praise.

This wasn't easy, since she was in diapers.

I would catch myself at baby group mid-fantasy, determined not to indulge in this nonsense. Pride, bragging, caring about meaningless baby milestones was absurd and I knew it.

And yet, that girl sure walked awfully early.

Just sayin'.

Thank God for my Western upbringing. It made me constantly aware of the gap between my craving for the rush, and the reality of a living, breathing, child whose emotional needs were more important and very different from mine. I fought the impulse to make her "excel" because I recognized this desire as an expression of my own neurotic tendencies. A tiger mother claiming that she can be cruel because happiness doesn't matter is committing the ultimate hypocrisy since she derives *her* happiness from the hard work and accomplishments of her children.

Luckily, Ithaca was a place where open displays of pretentiousness were frowned on. We mocked mothers who taught their toddlers to "read" and pitied their children. Not that there were many of these sorts of mothers. Lack of opportunity forced them out. Or, as in my case, kept them subdued.

Thus, when Hana turned three, we sent her to a little Waldorf "school" where she twirled with multi-colored scarves and coated herself in mud. The children would ask for more tofu, and the beautiful teacher, Sue, would smile gently and say, "Not until you finish your kale, sweetie."

There was no learning to read, which the Waldorf philosophy delayed until second grade for peculiar reasons I didn't understand, but also didn't care much about. Just so long as they let kids be kids, we all said to each other.

I wondered how many of the other mothers had secret plans for world domination held, barely, in check by a set of values that forbid parental tyranny? Or was I the only one afflicted with this insane desire for my infant to prove herself better than other infants?

We lived across the street from the local public elementary school, a progressive place that was highly regarded in our little world. When Hana was five, off she toddled, ready to start what would surely be her stellar academic career supervised by the dour, but (hopefully) competent Ms. Grace.

But meanwhile, the itch demanded to be scratched. What else should we be doing for our brilliant, gorgeous Hana? She danced a little at the local studio. Clearly, she excelled at dance, but I couldn't escape the suspicion that she mostly liked the sparkly, pink outfits. Also, I wasn't thrilled with the other mothers, who carried a heavy sadness about them that made me suspect that they had a secret closet stuffed with much, much (much) larger sparkly, pink costumes for themselves.

How about an instrument?

True, Hana's father and I were musically illiterate. My husband had grown up poor, the kind of poor where he got toothpaste for Christmas. He never played a note and couldn't read music. I grew up in a suburban middle-class Jewish home, so I played the piano badly and sporadically until I was twelve. I also somehow managed to keep at the viola through middle school, before I decided boys were much more fun.

But maybe Hana had some innate musical talent that neither one of her parents had bothered to develop. I researched and found my new hero—Shin'ichi Suzuki.

Mr. Suzuki believed there was no such thing as talent. Hard work and proper instruction could make anyone a musician.

I had a sneaky suspicion this might be important.

I loved Suzuki's theory of mastery learning: the student doesn't move on until each skill has been mastered completely. In this way, children learn at their own pace, with excellence achieved at every level. With skill, teaches Suzuki, comes happiness and beauty.

Amen to that! I wanted to live my whole life by this theory. Slow, patient, gentle progress toward mastery. Maybe one day, by this theory, I could do my own taxes, learn to dance, to sing. Anything would be possible!

Mastery learning is based on Mr. Suzuki's observation that all Japanese children learn Japanese. Suzuki thought that this was an amazing achievement. Japanese was a difficult, complicated, nuanced language, he observed. But even the dullest Japanese child can master it. Why? Because they start young, go at their own pace, are constantly praised, and gently corrected. Why can't we teach music this way? Forget reading music—who needs it? That can come when the child is ready. After all, we don't teach children to read books until they've become fluent speakers, why teach them to read music until they've become fluent musicians?

Not reading music, but memorizing it *naturally*, was a vital component of Suzuki education, its core. I heard small children around the halls and classrooms of the Suzuki Institute beg to be taught to read music and be rebuffed. Isn't it so refreshing, so inspiring to hear a child beg to learn a difficult skill?

I was in.

My husband withheld judgment.

"Hana, do you want to play the violin?" I asked.

"Yes!" she cried happily. "What's a violin?"

Chapter 4

by Hana: What I Love/What I Hate

I was supposed to write about Suzuki. But I thought that was boring. Plus, I barely remember Suzuki, except for my teacher Mrs. Butter's extra-long fingers, which were *wonderfully* creepy.

Right out of a Tim Burton movie.

I love Tim Burton movies.

What you love is important. If you live your own life, you know what you love. If you live to please your parents, your list of what you love will show it.

So here's a list of what I love and what I hate. If you're a kid and you can't make a list like this, then you spend too much time doing something boring.

You better get on it.

Because if you don't know what you love, how can you know what to do with your life? Will you listen to your mother and father tell you what you should love? What you should do?

A little story—just to make my mother happy. (See, tigers aren't awful. We can be cute and cuddly when we choose.) I have a friend who can't make choices. He's a major pain in the butt. He can't choose an ice cream flavor—and then when he does choose—yep, you guessed it—vanilla. He can't order off a menu, can't do anything.

Once, we were at this party and his mother was there, too. His mom wouldn't eat any of the food because it was too unhealthy. She had brought her own food.

Yeah—to a party.

Anyway, this kid eats the party food and is having a grand old time, then he looks over at his mother. She's ignoring him, but in a mean way that lets him know she's ignoring him on purpose. So he goes over to her all moping and asks for a bite of her salad. She lets him have a bite, like she's letting him into Disney World.

"Oh, Mom," he says. "That is so much better than all that other expensive, unhealthy food."

Yeah right.

Kiss ass.

Bet he can't make a list of what he loves. He's too busy pretending to love what she loves. And if you do that too long, you'll just end up lost and no one will want to hang out with you and they'll be right because you kind of suck.

Make a list. Then study it and make sure it's about you and no one else, especially her. (Hint: if a bunch of stuff on your list might also be on your mom's list, you're in big trouble. Go re-read my last chapter, then try again.)

List of things I Love:

Unicorns, cupcakes, rainbows, buttons, Martha Stewart, bright yellow, turquoise, nail polish, accessories, pink, cake, stuffed animals, knitting, sewing, crocheting, embroidery, making cool stuff out of boring stuff, cats, smoothies, tea parties, bright colors, cookies, tootsie pops, Dwight from The Office, IKEA, crepes, clocks, ice tea, tutus, thrift shops, sparkly things, baking.

List of things I hate:

Loud noises, pinks that are too orange, the smell of oranges, the TV show Degrassi, computers, The Pogues, sound effects, unnecessary hand gestures, when people too old do stuff that's too young, sports, sports on a computer, basketball shoes, manpris (capris on men), sneakers (except Converse), black eyeliner (also known as "stuff for people who want to look like cows"), "that's what he said/she said," plastic princess crowns, peace signs (ever notice that the meanest people wear them?), inappropriately named nail polish ("Mom, can I have Sex on the Beach?"), yellowed whites, when someone's pants don't fit, being late, people who smell funny, purple with silver, spelling, South Park, roman numerals.

Chapter 5

by Diana: Twinkle Twinkle Little Star

When Hana started playing her elfin violin, the disturbing competitive feelings I had tried to squash rushed to the forefront. I felt ridiculously proud carrying her little violin back and forth from the car every Tuesday, hoping people would see. *Look at me, carrying a violin for my little prodigy! Over here! Woo-hoo for me! I am so cultured! My child is so advanced. So how is Kindermusic? Fun?*

What was it about motherhood that made me, a person who looked down on goody-goody, boring, conventional people, suddenly want to prove my—I mean my child's—worth through goody-goody, conventional pursuits? Was this my rebellion against all the scarf-twirling going on around me? To be a rebel in Ithaca was to be a hard ass?

I didn't have time to analyze my motives because we had a lot of music to master. For months, we dutifully practiced every day and trotted off every week to the Suzuki Institute for Hana's lesson.

After months of this, the group classes were added on. They quickly became Hana's weekly torture.

"I'm so pleased group class is finally beginning," Mrs. Butter, Hana's teacher, said. "She'll progress so much faster with the added lesson!" Since Hana had been playing *Twinkle Twinkle Little Star* for eight long, tedious months, progress sounded good.

So there we were one stunning fall morning. Eight children aged three to seven stood in two lines. Their bows moved together like the New York Philharmonic while eight parents watched from metal folding chairs. The $3,000 seats, I called them. Like most tiger parent pursuits, Suzuki instruction was pay-to-play.

The other mothers and fathers were on the edge of their seats, serious and worried, their tongues clucking. They gave the disturbing impression that they carried two cases, one for the itsy-bitsy violin, and the other, velvet-lined, in which to pack the child until next week's lesson.

What were we doing here in this stultified place, having our children pretend they were miniature concert violinists?

After the warm up "games," Mrs. Butter played single notes. The children shouted out, "Bach's Minuet Number One!" or, "Gavotte!" guessing the mystery tune. Hana and I listened and sang along with the CD of the Suzuki repertoire every night, our daily prayers for a life filled with happiness, success, beauty, and mastery. Yet Hana (and I) still couldn't guess what the four-year-olds knew, sometimes even before Mrs. Butter's bow touched the strings. The little imps watched her fingerings, so they knew what note she would play before she played it.

Suck ups.

My mind wandered. *I wish I had a book. I wish I had coffee. I wish I had a Bloody Mary. I wonder if any of these mothers want to skip out of here for brunch?* When I refocused, seven children were playing *Twinkle Twinkle Little Star* and one child was crouched on the floor weeping.

That would be Hana.

I whisked her out of the room to the small hallway, all eyes on us. It sometimes felt like Suzuki students didn't read music so as to better observe the humiliation of their peers.

Hana's tiny body collapsed into my arms. "C-can't do it." Her red, swollen eyes spilled hot tears.

"First, yes you can," I told her. She hadn't "mastered" *Twinkle Twinkle*, but she was well on her way. Sort of. I supposed. What did I know about music, after all?

True, most of the six-year-old kids who had started with her were on to *Go Tell Aunt Rhody* or one of the other more advanced songs in the First Suzuki Violin Book, but not all of them.

Wait—all of them.

I continued to ramble, trying to hide that I was angry and upset at her for not learning the damn song after so many months of weekly lessons and daily practice. "Second, who cares? No one cares if you miss a note or get lost. This is just for fun." I was fighting back my own tears. Why the hell could Julia Lennon, our neighbor and baby group buddy born three days *after* Hana, play *Twinkle Twinkle* and Hana couldn't? Almost a year on one song? While this was normal, even fast for the four-year-olds, Hana was *old*. She was six! What was wrong with this child?

"I hate *Twinkle*," Hana moaned.

Yeah, well just wait for Go Tell Aunt Rhody, I wanted to shout at her. You think that's gonna be a picnic?

I wanted to whisper, *I hate fucking Twinkle, too.*

Instead I said, "Just because it looks like the other kids are playing *Twinkle*, it doesn't mean they're really playing it. Or playing it well. I heard Julia squeaking." I was lying.

Hana watched me carefully, her enormous blue eyes still red with tears.

I bungled on. "And you know what? She didn't care! Why? Because she was just having fun!"

But I hit the word "fun" too hard and Hana glared at me, her tiny fists curled in rage and frustration.

The child may not have known a flat F-sharp when she heard one, but she had perfect pitch when it came to her mother.

#

It wasn't that we didn't practice. We did. But our practice sessions were torture. It was dull to play the same thing over and over, and Hana wanted to play outside, play with her dolls, play with her neighbors. The only success we ever had with the violin was a game we called "Kill Mrs. Butter."

Mrs. Butter, Hana's teacher, was a prim, proper woman who did everything with precise deliberation until I wanted to pull out my hair and scream at her, *I'm paying you a dollar a minute lady, would you please get on it?*

This, I suppose, wasn't very Eastern of me.

Our game wasn't kind. It wasn't respectful. But it worked. I'd pretend to be Mrs. Butter, prim and upright. Hana would slowly kill me with awful, screechy playing. I'd fall to the floor, stricken dead by a bad-music-induced heart attack. Rigor mortis set in until I was revived with an especially lovely rendition of *Twinkle Twinkle Little Star*.

I knew this was not what Mr. Suzuki intended by "joyful playing." Especially after Hana marched out one session, leaving my corpse stiff on the floor, delighted with her very first musical accomplishment.

"She sucks," I told my husband after a particularly dreadful practice.

"Of course she sucks," he said. "She's my child. And no offense, yours. Also, remember, she's six. What did you expect?"

Genius, potential, hope, love, beauty, proof that she was special and by extension that I was special. Was that too much to ask? "Some of the kids are really good. You can tell who has potential and who's a disaster."

"That's why they call it talent."

"But Suzuki says—"

"Suzuki is a load of crap," he suggested. "Every Japanese person can speak Japanese my ass. Look at English—a pretty tough language, too. You have your lispers, your stutterers, your mutes. There are your mumblers, your Tourette syndrome sufferers. Don't forget the ex-presidents who say *you misunderestimated me.* There are the greeting card poem writers and all the people who actually buy the damn cards and cry over them. But those same people won't read *Lolita* because it's got bad language. To a majority of humans language is nothing. They have no feel for it. No sense of rhythm at all. They miss the magic completely. Most people are so inarticulate, so grossly insensitive to the language they use every day, it's a wonder they get by. Come and read a few of my students' papers sometime if you want proof. And these kids are supposedly the cream of the crop. Excellence takes inborn passion and—dare I say it?—talent."

He had a point.

Still, we kept at it. But no matter how hard Hana tried she couldn't get through *Twinkle*. It was becoming a form of insanity. It was arduous. It was as boring as watching paint dry. When she played I thought about kamikaze pilots, crashing their planes into aircraft carriers. I thought about manga and anime cartoons, the characters overwrought with giant, compliant, dewy eyes. What was up with the Japanese?

We quit Suzuki after a year of not even coming close to mastering *Twinkle Twinkle Little Star.*

I was consumed with shame and rage.

Why can't she play *Twinkle?*

A few weeks later, Hana's first grade teacher pulled me aside in the hall after school. "Hana's not learning to read as quickly as we'd like."

"What was that?" I was surrounded by bustling parents and children, each one more perfect and happier than the next. Surely I'd misheard her. *Not learning to bead, not learning to feed...*

The teacher repeated what she'd said, adding a few details that I was too stunned to take in. Everyone around me was smiling, happy, healthy, perfect.

The teacher was staring at me. It was my turn to speak. "Um. Okay. Right. So. What do we do?"

The teacher threw out vague notions of this and that.

You should know about this little Twinkle *issue.*

No way could I form the words.

I had come to a parenting crossroads: Was I going to indulge in my fantasies and make Hana succeed as a master violinist and ace student, no matter the cost? Or was it time to take a step back, a deep breath, and reevaluate?

Chapter 6

by Hana: Getting Married at IKEA

I'm going to get married at IKEA.

Every Tuesday night, my mom and I go to IKEA because it's near my brother Isaiah's soccer practice. Also, because we love IKEA.

A lot.

If you don't know what IKEA is, what's wrong with you?

It's a furniture store. But it's more than that. It's a paradise.

If you've never been, you really ought to go. Go now. I'll wait. Come back when you understand.

You back? Okay. Good. Now you know that it is one of the most awesome places on earth.

For my birthday this year, I got a $2.95 red, rubber spatula from their kitchen section. That's because Isaiah had soccer practice on my birthday and my father was out of town, so my birthday dinner was at IKEA, with my mom, who had forgotten to get me a present. She's kind of like that sometimes. She'll buy me pretty much anything I want any time I want, so when there's a special occasion, she thinks a red, $2.95 IKEA spatula makes perfect sense.

"Happy Birthday, Hon!"

Usually, we sit in the cafe and my mom drinks coffee and we eat a cheap, delicious dinner. I like the pasta and the wraps. My mom always says she doesn't want a Princess Cake, but then she eats mine. Believe me, you want a Princess Cake. Sometimes, I bring a friend and we run around. Mostly, I bring homework because we're always running straight from my viola lesson and I have a lot to get done.

It was during one of these trips that I told my mom that I had decided to get married at IKEA.

"What if the guy you want to marry doesn't want to get married at IKEA?" she asked, not looking up from her computer.

"Why would I ever marry a guy who wouldn't want to get married at IKEA?"

Ha. That got her to look up.

She blinked at me the way she sometimes does when she doesn't know what to say.

"We'd have the ceremony in the couch section," I said. I'd put a lot of thought into this. "So everyone would have a place to sit. Then we'd go to the cafe and everyone would get a tray and wait in line for Swedish meatballs with lingonberries. It would be the best wedding food ever. The band could be right there." I pointed to the toddler area. I don't enjoy little kids. No toddlers at my wedding.

"You'd need waiters."

"I guess. Okay. Waiters in blue and yellow," I said.

"Would strangers be shopping during the ceremony?" she asked.

"Sure, why not? But only dressed up people could come to the party in the cafe after."

"What about your grandfather? You know he'd be wearing the wrong thing and they might not let him in." My grandfather is notorious for not having such good dressing ideas. She paused. "Maybe we could send the guests bracelets along with the invitations, so we'd know who could get the free meatballs."

That wasn't a bad idea. "And if they forgot a gift, they could just buy something on the way from the ceremony to the reception." I was really getting excited about this. "I could have a whole collection of Spokas." Spokas are these great little night lights that change colors. I only have one, but you could cover a room in them, which would be a great idea.

Later, my mom wanted me to write my IKEA wedding idea for this book.

"No way," I said. "Someone will steal it. I want to be the first person to be married at IKEA."

"No one will steal it," she said, as if she had any clue what a bunch of strangers would do. "It's harder to steal ideas than you think, and if you hold back your ideas, the book won't be good."

"But how hard is it to get married at IKEA?" My mother is kind of dense sometimes. Anyone can get married anywhere.

She said, "Okay, what if we put this in: Dear Reader: If you steal my idea and get married at IKEA before I do, you have to invite me to the wedding as your guest of honor."

"Okay." I still wasn't happy.

But she was back at her computer.

"And I get to wear a wedding gown, too," I said.

"That might be pushing it."

"They stole my idea. They deserve to be punished."

"Punished?"

"I'll look better than them," I explained. I love wedding gowns. I know just about everything about them. I research them on the web.

"Okay. It's in. Deal?"

"Deal," I agreed.

But to anyone out there reading this: you better not get married at IKEA.

Chapter 7

by Diana: Why We Did Nothing

Hana's grandfather is a professor at Yale. He did awful in first grade. Therefore, a child who sucks at first grade could end up being a professor at Yale.

#

"Suzuki is awful," people say. People who know about these sorts of things. Musicians, as opposed to mothers of small children who badly want those children to be musicians and will pay any price to a person who promises they can make it so. "It's rare for a truly great musician to come out of the Suzuki Method. It's much too rigid."

I have no idea if this is true or not, but I enjoy the sentiment too much to try to find out.

#

I need a real job. I'm proofing English-language ads freelance for a Swiss ad agency, but it's dull, nothing to call a passion. My social life becomes my center.

"She's so conventional," a friend says about a mother on the playground one long, endless afternoon. In Ithaca, "conventional" was a terrible insult.

"I know," another mother says with disgust.

I realize that I'm becoming conventional. Nothing is more

conventional than my panicky urge to push my child into ultra-snooty pursuits. The violin? Really? What was I thinking? What would be next, cotillion? Water polo? I was never this kind of person. I can't let motherhood take my mojo.

I go home, open my computer, and type "Chapter One."

I'd always wanted to write a novel. It was about time I got started.

#

A boy from our baby group drops out of first grade to homeschool because he fights with the other children.

One down.

#

Albert Einstein didn't do well at school. Albert Einstein is a genius. Therefore, even geniuses don't always do well in school. (This Albert Einstein story is apparently a myth, but no worries. Like all myths, it served our purposes at the time.)

#

Two more children from our baby group struggle with reading. Was it all that vegan casserole, leaving protein imbalances and iron deficiencies in the blood? Or are reading and behavioral "issues" more ubiquitous than parents know? If I didn't know these mothers intimately, I'd have no idea their children were also imperfect.

They all look so perfect.

Who else has flaws?

Strike two more babes off the "normal" list.

#

Talk of the outdated school system trying to teach reading with the Whole Language method swirls around me. *It's those teachers. They're stuck in the seventies. So outdated. No one believes Whole Language is a good way to teach reading anymore. Uneducated teachers.*

Sheesh, they're almost as bad as those awful Suzuki teachers. Maybe even worse.

It's reassuring and a tremendous amount of fun to have someone to blame. The best thing about tiger parenting is that you always know best.

#

I finish my first manuscript and get seventeen rejections from agents. For every "no" that comes in, I send two more queries out.

#

Hana's other grandfather was slow to read. He faked it for years, he tells me, gleaning basic meaning from the words he could decipher.

They thought he was a speed reader because he scanned the pages so quickly and faked it so well. Now he's a doctor. Therefore, slow readers can fake it and become doctors.

Why had I never known this about my father?

#

Hana doesn't fail first grade. On the contrary, her report cards (no grades, just narrative) are stellar.

#

Hana decides to pick up the violin again in school.

I'm stunned, but she insists.

During the first lesson, her public school teacher (who does not make a dollar a minute and teaches twelve children at a time in the damp, dark school basement) sees she knows a great deal, and so teaches her a simple method of reading music. E1 means one finger on the E string, E2 means two fingers, and so on. He sends her home with a ream of pages covered in numbers and letters. Freed from the Suzuki ideology of memorization, armed with her new violin and her printed out melodies, she goes to her room and plays through *Hot Cross Buns* and *Row Row Row Your Boat*.

Then I hear it: *Twinkle* played perfectly, beautifully, musically, from beginning to end.

I come into her room, mouth agape.

She looks just as shocked. Then her mood shifts ominously. She eyes me with contempt. "Why didn't anyone tell me you could write it down?"

#

Hana learns to ski. She learns to ice skate. She learns to bike. She learns to swim. She has a best friend she adores.

A funny thing starts happening along the way: slowly, steadily, she learns to read.

#

A girl from baby group changes her name to "Charlie" and insists on wearing boys bathing trunks and no shirt to the town pool.

There goes another one, tumbling joyfully and fearlessly off the "normal" cart.

The mother of this little girl/boy couldn't care less. She goes along with a shrug and a nod of admiration for her child's bravery in the face of convention. I am in awe of this mother who accepts her child's swimwear so calmly and with such quiet grace. Yet, I can't help wonder again: are none of these children normal? Or is the myth of normal for people in sunnier towns, where the glare is so strong, no one can see the details of individuality? *Fight the Dominant Paradigm* is a common bumper sticker on the ancient green Subaru wagons tooling up and down the steep Ithacan hills. But there's not much to fight here, in this lovely, leafy, left-leaning town, where the light is low and everyone feels free to do as they please in the comfort of the shadows.

\#

Third grade.

Hana can't learn her times tables to save her life.

Oh no. Here we go again.

The tiger mother still pacing inside me wants to drill her into submission.

"My mother did that to me after first grade," a friend tells me.

"Did it work?" I'm itching to make flash cards, already dizzy from just imagining the heady aroma of sharpies—the smell of success. I've been battling this impulse for years now. *I can catch her up if I just work hard enough, if she just works hard enough. It's hard work and willpower that holds us back.* I want someone to give me permission to be this snarling, abusive, mean parent because, let's face it, I'm angry at her.

"I'm a doctor," my friend says.

"So it worked," I point out.

"Diana, I'm a forty-year-old woman still reliving the horror of my first grade summer. Yes, it worked. But I'd never wish it on anyone."

I hold my worst, basest impulses in check.

"No worries," Hana's decidedly anti-paradigm teacher says as we discuss the situation. "Some kids just can't memorize math facts. No reason to torture them." The teacher hands Hana a multiplication chart to tape into the front of her notebook.

I remember Suzuki. The torture, then the eventual obvious solution: *why didn't anyone tell me you could write it down?*

I love public school.

\#

Some book called *Harry Potter and the Half-Blood Prince* comes out. It's 642 pages long. Kids carry it around like a badge of honor, but Hana thinks the cover looks "stupid" and she "doesn't care" if it's too daunting to read.

I've heard of this Harry Potter sensation, but it doesn't appeal to me either, so we don't give it another thought.

"What'd you do at recess today?" I ask one gorgeous fall afternoon.

"We played Harry Potter."

My heart sinks into my stomach. "Oh?" Must get reading tutor; must read *Harry Potter* to her out loud; must tackle this problem head-on and stop pretending it's not a problem.

"I was Hermione," she says. "She's the smartest wizard."

"How do you know that?" I ask.

She rolls her eyes at me. "Everyone knows that."

#

One of the mothers I admire most, a ridiculously famous professor of physics, has non-identical twins. Sally excels at everything: school, friends, looks. Beth is quiet, plain, struggling at school, alone in so many ways. This poor girl, Beth, has just returned from a camping trip during which she has managed to get poison ivy on every inch of her body. She's lying prone and miserable on the couch, socks taped over her hands to keep her from scratching while her beautiful sister dashes off with friends.

"Bye, Mom! Bye Beth!" Sally calls, not entirely kindly.

We're in the kitchen, drinking coffee while Hana and Beth discuss the joys of scratching in the other room.

"It's like cake," Hana says.

"Chocolate cake," Beth replies, moaning.

"I can't imagine the sibling rivalry you must deal with," I whisper to the mother.

"It's bad," the mother admits. "Poor Sally."

"Sally?" I'm not sure I heard right. Beth is the oozing twin on the couch.

"Peaking too early is a tragedy that most kids can never overcome. I see it in my Cornell students all the time. Brilliant, but without the intellectual curiosity and the grit to be real scientists. They've either never had it, like Sally. Or they lost it because they've always been told what to do and how to think by overbearing parents. Beth, she explores, goes off the path, you know? She has the right impulses." The mother pulls up the sleeve of her shirt. Her arm is covered in a ghostly, swirled scar. "Poison ivy," she says. "1972. Over my entire body." She shoots me a mischievous smile.

Poor Sally.

#

I finish my second manuscript.

This time, after only twelve rejections, the phone starts ringing.

I get to pick my agent from several offers.

#

The professor who left Harvard to teach at SUNY Binghamton because he couldn't stand the snobbery? Just another neighbor who grows excellent heirloom tomatoes.

The "slacker" from around the corner who cross-country skis down the middle of the road on his homemade roller-skis? Oh, he's no slacker. He's famous. Didn't you know he writes for Marvel comics?

Did you see Brian's new book on the cover of the *New York Times Book Review*? And you thought he was just another hippie who bought that house we looked at but passed up because it was too small? Just like John in the tiny house on the corner with homemade bookshelves who just had his new novel excerpted in *Harper's*. Or the literary agent who lives to pick raspberries. She has huge, best-selling clients whose names you know. She has written and published her own novel with a prestigious New York publisher. But what really turns her on? Baking for her friends with those raspberries.

Most of our friends live on the edge of poverty. They have no health insurance. They are wildly successful at low-paying endeavors. They have bands. They paint. They write. They travel. They have ponds that ice over in the winter to skate on.

They have insanely brilliant children with nothing to prove.

They are very happy people.

They are buckets of fun.

#

My shiny new agent can't sell my manuscript. "There aren't that many editors who buy this sort of thing," she warns me.

Meanwhile, my old creative director from the last ad agency I worked at dreams up a little ad campaign for MasterCard. "Two tickets, twenty-eight dollars. Two hot dogs, two popcorns, and two sodas, eighteen dollars...Real conversation with your eleven-year-old son...priceless."

He becomes very famous and very, very well-paid overnight. He had been my creative director, one of my biggest champions. I could have gone with him to McCann...I could have been there...

Why did I ever leave advertising? Why did I ever leave Manhattan? What was I doing in this cold, grey place trying to do something I wasn't good at? Something that might not even be doable by a person like me? I should have stuck with what I knew. Something that paid real money. Something that wasn't so nebulous, so risky.

It was scary out here in do-what-you-love land. Failure was getting to me. Nothing is harder than failing over and over again. Trying to do something risky is humiliating. It's humbling.

I try to convince myself that I had ever been any good at anything. Had I?

#

A crew of neighborhood kids fill up our sandbox with water from the hose. This isn't just any sandbox. It's a seven-by-five-foot, two-feet-deep frame that past owners of our house built as a raised garden bed. It sat dormant for years before we moved in, and since I'm not a gardener, we filled it with fifteen hundred pounds of play sand.

The kids play until dusk in the sand, their games complicated, important, and absorbing. Hours pass. Days. Weeks. Months. Years. The game stretches on and on, morphing and changing as they morph and change.

I look out the back window. Hana is preparing "cakes" in her "bakery" for the next day's morning rush. Isaiah and Silas are harvesting berries and sticks that they mash into a messy, mushy mess.

Everyone has a job they love but me.

#

April 12th, 2005, 3:32 PM, the phone rings.

My agent tells me I've sold two manuscripts in a two-book deal to A Major New York Publisher.

Leaving advertising—negative $100,000 a year.

Struggling for years to learn the craft of fiction writing—negative $10,000 a year.

Finally after years of work and disappointment, selling my first two novels—priceless.

Chapter 8

by Hana: Life in the Sandbox

I ran the bakery. We had to make hundreds of cakes everyday for everyone in the town. It took a lot of time and you had to be very, very careful. Isaiah and Silas were usually my assistants. I'd send them into the bushes to gather berries and sticks and things for decorations. Then we'd mush the berries to color the icing, and break up the sticks to add decorations. When Sylvia would come, she'd help me in the kitchen. I forget the rest of the story, but there were always stories about whose wedding we were baking for or whose birthday.

There were a lot of birthday parties.

The birthday cakes were the best to make. They had to be huge and they were very important. Sometimes, they'd be for very old people, which was fun because we'd have to put on hundreds of candles. They were really sticks, of course. We'd "light" them with juice from the berries.

We'd build villages along the rivers. Everyone had houses, but some houses were bigger than others. It depended how important you were in the village. They got destroyed all the time. There were a lot of floods. I loved to rake my fingers through the cold water rushing through the hot sand, destroying everything. The sand felt like a beautiful princess's long, silky hair.

My favorite times were when the cats would come. They'd sit on the side of the sandbox while we worked. They didn't like the water, though. They also didn't like to be decorated when they fell asleep in the sun, but they'd let us do it anyway, berries and twigs down their backs.

They looked like beautiful little cakes until they opened their eyes, got up, shook off, and walked away.

Chapter 9

by Diana: To the Moon

When Hana turned nine, everything and nothing changed. That is, everything was exactly as it had always been, but we left the easygoing paradise of Ithaca behind and moved to the suburbs of Philadelphia.

It didn't take long before the teachers at Hana's new school told us The Story.

What's The Story? First, a warning. When they start telling you The Story, you know you're in for something you most definitely aren't prepared for, even if it's been right in front of your face for years. When they tell you The Story, you know you're about to lose any control that you thought you had as a parent.

It's called "Welcome to Holland" and it was written in 1987 by Emily Pearl Kingsley. Ms. Kingsley wrote The Story to explain what it's like having a child who is different from what the parents expected.

It goes something like this: Having a baby is like planning a fabulous trip to Italy. But when the plane touches down, you find yourself in Holland. You're pissed, because you wanted to go to Italy. Now you need new guidebooks. You're going to have to deal with Dutch people and their lax drug laws and silly wooden shoes. Meanwhile, all your friends are whooping it up in Italy, having the grand old time that you had planned for yourself.

The moral is that if you take a deep breath, you'll see that Holland kind of rocks. Sure, it might be quaint and quiet, but Dutch people speak excellent English with adorable accents; Amsterdam has free, bright yellow bikes you can borrow and ride around all afternoon; and, smoking a little pot here and there isn't actually so bad.

Okay, so I'm taking big liberties with Ms. Kingsley's story—search it on the Internet for the real version.[2] It's very sweet, heartwarming, and helpful. But Ms. Kingsley's point stands: get over your obsession with Italy, and you might find amazing things in Holland. Maybe Holland will end up even better than Italy in many meaningful and important ways. Go with the flow, and you'll find happiness. That's what having a kid is all about.

Looking back now, years later, knowing how things ended up, I can tell you that Hana's story isn't about conventional Italy or quiet Holland. If I'd known then what I know now, I'd have stopped those well-meaning educators mid-story and said (with apologies to Ms. Kingsley), "Don't tell me where you think my daughter is going. I'll tell you Hana's story. It's called, 'Welcome To The Moon' and it goes like this":

Having a baby is like planning a trip to Italy. After months of eager preparation, it's time to go. But the plane mysteriously turns into a spaceship and next thing you know, the stewardess is saying, "Welcome to the Moon."

"What?" you cry. "I'm supposed to be in Italy. All my life I've dreamed of going to Italy."

But there's been a change in the flight plan, a paradigm shift in the very fiber of reality, and there's no way back. You have landed on the moon.

So you get off the plane—spaceship—and you don't know where you are or where you're going. It feels dangerous. It's gaspingly confusing. It's full of people—wait, are those people or aliens? Or worse, teenagers? You can't be sure and there's no time to get your bearings. Creatures with multi-colored hair float past doing the backstroke in zero gravity. (Yep, teenagers.) You're scared to death. You want to go out and buy new guide books—but there are no guide books. This is all too new.

Just when you're sure you're doomed in this strange land, there is your child. She's doing back flips over your head and eating Space Goo and taking notes on alien fashion trends to tweet to her friends on some gadget that you still don't know how to work no matter how many times she tried to show you.

---

[2] http://www.our-kids.org/Archives/Holland.html

"Mom, I can't believe you wanted to go to Italy. Compared to the moon, Italy is totally lame."

There's a telescope by the big crater. You look through it and back to earth and you see all those people in Italy, where you were supposed to be, eating spaghetti and throwing pennies into the Trevi Fountain thinking that they are experiencing something truly excellent. You train the telescope on Holland. It looks lovely, but quiet—a nice place to rest after your moon expedition.

Then you look out over the intense lunar landscape; you look at the creatures floating by, the breathtaking views, and you know you've arrived at exactly the right place. You know that those folks in Italy and Holland have no idea what they're missing and they never will. *Because you're on the frickin' moon.*

You could never have imagined this world, because it wasn't yours to imagine. This world is the future and it's not about you; it's about your kid. She's the future. She's the one who somehow, when you weren't looking, made this journey possible.

If you let it happen, you'll get to tag along for the ride of your life.

If you're overbearing and are sure that you know best, you'll hoof it back to Italy or maybe Holland no matter what it takes and demand a refund. You'll probably even consider suing and will have many friends who encourage you to do so. In fact, you're probably a lawyer, so no problem.

But that's the story I'd tell now, years later, in hindsight.

Then, I was the mother of a bewildered fourth grader at a new school, and I let them do what I'd learn never to ever let anyone do, especially myself: underestimate Hana.

So I sat quietly, listening and nodding while the well-meaning educators of Hana's new school finished their version of The Story.

Then they told me that they just got Hana's fourth grade placement results. "She's at a second grade level in math."

"Oh. Yeah. That. She's usually allowed a chart," I said.

They squinted their eyes at me. "A chart?"

"She has her math facts written down. It works great."

"Oh. No. Mrs. Holquist, That's not how we do things here."

Houston, we have a problem.

Chapter 10

by Hana: What Did You Do Today—Part I

We were dropping my uncle off in downtown Philadelphia for the bus to New York. It was a freezing windy day. The bus was on a bridge and we watched a guy's hat fly off his head and under the bridge.

It was a really nice hat.

The guy and his friends looked over the bridge, but they had to get on the bus because it was leaving soon.

"Poor guy," my mother says. "That was a nice hat."

"We should get it for him," I say.

My mother frowns. She looks at her watch. "The bus is leaving in six minutes. I don't even know what's down there." It's a strange part of town, by the train station and a giant abandoned post office.

"We should try," I say.

So we drive around, trying to find a way under the bridge. Finally, we get there. Turns out there's a huge, dirty, chained up parking lot down there. Half parking lot, half construction zone.

"I can't drive in," my mother says.

She hates the cold. I can tell she doesn't want to get out of the car.

"It was a really nice hat." We can still see the bus on the bridge.

We get out. We have to climb over the chains and over huge piles of dirty snow the plows have pushed into mounds. When we get to the edge of the parking lot, we climb over a huge snowdrift.

There are hundreds of hats.

We just stand and stare.

"Wow," my mom says.

Wow is right.

Most of the hats have obviously been down here for a long, long time. I imagine all the people walking over the bridge overhead, their hats flying off. Everyone's in such a rush, no time to come under the bride to get a hat back. You could open a Phillies or Eagles hat store with all the sports hats. Old lady hats, too. Little kid hats.

"We're never going to find—" my mother starts.

"There it is!"

The man's hat is off to the side, still in the street. It hasn't blown into the sea of hats yet, like it's also paralyzed by this amazing sight.

We grab the guy's hat. It's just a little wet from the snow, but otherwise fine. We run back to the car, my mother huffing and puffing behind me.

We screech back to the bridge. The bus is still there.

"I can't drive down the street. It's one way the wrong way. You have to run," my mother says.

I'm on it.

"Don't get on the bus!" she yells after me. "I don't have enough gas to follow you to New York."

I race down the street and bang on the door. The driver opens it. I tell him that someone on the bus lost their hat.

He looks at me like I'm nuts.

Then his look changes into mad when I don't leave.

He takes the hat, then turns to the back of the bus.

"Anyone lose a hat?"

But I can see that everyone's got their earphones on. Hardly anyone even looks up. My uncle's on the bus, but he doesn't see me and I can't see him.

When I get back to the car my mom asks, "So? Was it awesome? Were they thrilled to get their hat back?"

"I don't know." I tell her the story.

"Sometimes it's the doing that counts," she says. But I can tell she's disappointed. I am too. We pull onto the highway.

I don't think that it's the doing that counts. I think it was seeing hundreds of lost hats under that bridge that counts. That was an amazing sight.

Later, they move the bus stop to the side of the train station and I'm a little bummed. I wonder if anyone will ever see the hat graveyard again. Does anyone even walk over that old, abandoned bridge?

I wonder if that guy ever got his hat back.

Chapter 11

by Diana: Why We Did Something

Hana had always struggled with math, but it had never affected her personality before. Bad at math had meant bad at math. In the Ithaca schools, a significant percentage of the kids couldn't speak English. Then there were the handful or so bouncing off the walls with undiagnosed (or diagnosed but ignored) attention deficit issues. There were the kids raised in astounding poverty. And, the cherry on top, there were the children of non-repentant eccentrics. Some kids were mix and match, some even all of the above. *You can't do three times eight? Twenty-four. I just had my vestigial gills removed? Wanna see the scar?*

In the wealthy, heavily medicated, homogeneous suburbs of Philadelphia, bad at math made you a freak. Even if a child was bad at math, parents certainly wouldn't risk letting such a shocking deformity show. Tutors could take care of that. Very, very expensive tutors. We were pitifully naive about the façade we were expected to maintain.

Hana was suffering the academic and social consequences.

"Guess she'll need some extra help," I said to the teachers and the counselors who had delivered the news of Hana's substandard test scores. Hana's teachers in Ithaca had always rolled with the diversity of their classrooms with grace and creativity. No big deal.

Here, they stared back blankly.

The counselor patiently explained the situation to me. "Mrs. Holquist, she can't qualify for extra help unless she has an officially diagnosed learning disability."

"Okay, so how do we get one of those?"

"She'll have to apply for testing."

"Super."

"If we start now, which we can't because it takes a while to get everything scheduled, then the tests can take months."

Months? Her teacher sent her to the back of the room every day during math lessons with second-grade worksheets while her fourth grade class moved on without her. It was humiliating, and the stress was taking its toll. She wept every morning, begging me not to make her go to school.

What was wrong with these people?

When I told other parents our troubles, they would say, "You need the name of a good lawyer." Or, "You're not going to let the school test her! You must hire your own private learning specialist." Then they'd slip me a business card of their neighbor or their brother-in-law or of their own private business as a "learning specialist." Turns out Hana wasn't such a freak after all. There was an elaborate industry in place, ready to spring into action for the right price.

Strangely, this industry wasn't just for the kids who were struggling. A certain kind of parent tried to get their perfectly average kids diagnosed with learning differences so they could get expensive extra help and mandated extra time on standardized tests. Average wasn't good enough for these hyper parents. But the schools couldn't afford expensive services for everyone.

When the extra help was denied, parents sued.

"It's a very litigious community," a father told me as gorgeous, well-kept children walked in straight, single file lines down the halls of their pristine, award-winning school. "The schools have to protect their resources for the kids who truly need them. So you see why they can't just put Hana in the program."

The daily tears, the nightly misery, the second-grade-level math results weren't enough. We needed more numbers.

In other words—the irony!—we needed math.

Hiring our own specialist to fight for math help caused an entirely different sort of numbers problem: money. It would cost thousands of dollars that we didn't have to get the tests done privately. We didn't even want to think about getting started on the lawyers. One of my friends very generously and with the utmost seriousness offered to sit in on the school meetings with us and pretend to be our lawyer. She was a book publisher, but she owned nice suits, she told us with a perfectly straight face. Plus, her husband was a lawyer, so she knew how to fake it.

I had no idea what anyone was talking about. All I knew was that this monstrously uncreative teacher in this supposedly stellar school district had no capacity for dealing with Hana, who was rapidly deteriorating. We had to literally drag her to school. It wasn't just the math, although most of her anxiety revolved around that. She didn't understand anything about this new school.

I should have known we were going to have problems before we had gotten started. "Mommy," she had whispered to me as we had sat with name tags marked "visitor" in the back of her soon-to-be classroom a few months before we moved to town. "What is wrong with the kids here?"

I knew exactly what she meant. All the kids were sitting in neat rows, paying attention. In Ithaca, this only happened when the teacher brought in a lung and heart from a deer she'd found still warm on the side of the road so she could let the kids pass a marble from one organ to the next.

Okay, it didn't even happen then.

In Ithaca, there were certain kids you literally couldn't get out of the trees after school. "Joey, get out of that tree. You know you're not allowed up there." Joey would scowl down at the brave parent who dared challenge him and growl, "Make me." We called them the feral children. But here, no one was feral. After getting to know their parents better, I learned that they were either naturally civilized or heavily medicated.

Here after school no one even looked at the trees. A line of SUVs waited outside the playground with engines running to better heat or cool the little scholars while they were whisked off to after-school activities or math tutors or manicures or the ubiquitous orthodontist. Here, Hana was considered the feral child.

She was different, even before her math issues.

Being different was the kiss of death.

Hana didn't have close friends in her new school. She didn't like the teachers and they didn't seem to like her very much either. She didn't understand the culture and when she did understand it, she was repulsed. But all that stuff was hard to fix.

Please don't make me go. I hate that place. They're so mean. I can't do anything right there.

Next to this, math seemed easy.

I had endless conversations with the peppy, hapless school

counselor. Just about every employee in this school was young, perky, and exceptionally well groomed (the average teacher's salary in our district was $80,000). It wasn't just the teachers who looked flawless. It was hard not to stare at all the women's hair in this town. In Ithaca, most of my friends were going salt-and-pepper gray. Here, every middle-aged woman had the highlighted, bouncy hair I usually associated with extremely lucky seven-year-olds. I vowed never to dye my hair. I would live here, but I'd never give in to the conventions of this stunted place with its dubious values.

Was I getting my mojo back finally?

"How did they handle Hana's anxiety issues in her old school?" the counselor asked.

"She didn't have anxiety issues in her old school," I said, badly wanting to add that she wasn't tortured in her old school with work she couldn't possibly do by adults who seem to have lost every ounce of their creativity.

Finally, the state-sponsored testing began.

Week after week, Hana was pulled out of class by specialists for a barrage of tests: seeing, hearing, speaking—everything you could imagine, and a lot you couldn't possibly.

In January, her hatred of her ineffective teacher and her mistrust of the exceptionally well-dressed but unresponsive adults around her permanently established, we had the results. I couldn't wait to hear them. Finally, we'd know what was up with *Twinkle*. We'd know why she couldn't spell. Why she couldn't do three times goddamn three. At the time, I didn't stop to reflect that I still counted out my times tables on my fingers or that we already knew the solution to the *Twinkle* "problem" was to write the darn song down.

We didn't bring a lawyer to the meeting, although we were tempted to ask my father, a psychiatrist, to sit in as our "specialist" to have another body with credentials on our side.

The number of people from the school district at the table was obscene. The principal, the guidance counselor, the district psychologist, Hana's teacher, the special ed teacher, the student teacher, the speech specialist, and others I can't remember who I'd never see again.

Wow, I thought. This is going to be good.

After countless hours, thousands of dollars, and untold manpower, here we all were to hear the results.

The school psychologist had us sign endless documents. Then she cleared her throat, riffled through her papers, and declared, "Hana is eligible for service. She has a learning disability."

"What is it?" I asked, breathless with anticipation. This was the joy of science—of all that math paying off. They had located the specific problem that prevented my daughter from achieving her destiny. They held the secret in that stack of endless pages still left to sign, the path to fixing everything and getting Hana into Harvard after all.

Yale would be fine.

"She is more intelligent than her performance indicates."

"And—?" I asked.

"And that is the result."

"What's the result?"

"Mrs. Holquist, that's the definition of a learning difference. She tests exceptionally high for intelligence, but she underperforms at the specific tasks we ask of her in math. Therefore, she is eligible for help with math."

They went on for a while, but that was pretty much it. We had lost precious months for that. If Hana were only mildly intelligent, would she not have gotten help? I didn't dare ask. She was brilliant and she was in. That was all that mattered.

Now Hana was pulled out of class for math (as bad as her spelling was, she never qualified for help with language skills).

Now Hana had math class with just a couple of kids taught by excellent, highly trained teachers. We'd been handed the keys to the magic kingdom. We were back in the America I knew and loved, the one that accepted different styles, different paces, different modalities.

We had escaped our suburban nightmare.

Or had we?

I felt that itch again—the one that had made me hand a violin to a six-year-old. Anything was possible. You just had to decide what you wanted, work hard enough, and it would be yours. I mean, your child's.

I went to hear one of my favorite local writers speak at a nearby bookshop. "This is the Main Line, Baby! Get your roots done!" she cried, and we all laughed knowingly.

It was intoxicating, this drive to make yourself the best you could be.

The next day, I went to a salon to see about dyeing my hair.

Chapter 12

by Hana: Math Facts

I remember the testing. I was excited at first, because we got to go into a little room where the copier was, and I had always wondered what was in that room.

But there was just a copier.

They gave me hearing tests that were so boring, I was afraid I would fail them because I kept spacing out.

You could tell that most of the tests were for kids with serious problems. They'd show me pictures of four fruits. Which one starts with an "A?" they'd ask. "Um, the apple?" I'd say. "Good, Hana!" They'd say it like I was five.

I was in fourth grade. Did they really think I was that dumb? Was I that dumb?

Sometimes, the tests were so boring, the teacher would say, "You're not listening are you?"

"Oh, no," I'd say. "I'm listening." Then I'd make some stuff up to pretend I'd been listening and they'd say, "Good, Hana!"

Uh-huh.

They should have given my teacher the hearing tests, because she didn't hear very well. It was so unfair for the kids, because she never knew half of what was going on. You learned to stand on one side of her and shout so she could hear you, which of course meant that you also learned that she couldn't hear you on the other side. So kids would stand on her bad side and say stuff that they shouldn't.

Some part of her probably knew that she was being teased, so she got mean.

I hated school.

I missed Ithaca. In Ithaca, my third-grade teacher took us all to sleep over at her house. She had a llama and a horse. She tapped the sugar maple trees in her woods, then invited us to come to help her and her husband boil the sap into syrup over huge fires down by the lake.

She made us hot cocoa.

She gave each of us our very own spelling lists, with carefully chosen words just for us.

She was the kind of teacher with two good ears, but it didn't matter because she heard stuff you didn't even need to say out loud.

After they finally finished with all the tests, they let me leave the classroom whenever it was math time. I had a new, great teacher named Mrs. Pine, who knew how to teach math. She was really nice.

That made school a lot better, even if most kids still ignored me.

Every single girl in my class had long hair. Really. I swear.

I wanted to cut my hair, but my mom was against it.

I didn't know why, but I still wanted to. I didn't want to be like them. They were all the same. They dressed the same, talked the same, did the same kind of stuff (jazz dancing, soccer, swimming). The meaner you were, the more popular you were.

It was kind of scary how mean they could be to each other.

They mostly ignored me.

That was okay. I didn't want to be a part of it.

But if you weren't a part of it, what were you?

I'd stare in the mirror and picture myself with short hair.

I thought it would look pretty good.

Chapter 13

by Diana: The Coping Cat

Now that Hana was on track with math, we could take a deep breath and relax.

Or could we?

An old friend of Hana's came from Ithaca came to visit. While the girl's mother and I caught up on the playground, I watched Hana swinging slowly with her buddy. They were too big for the swing set, so their feet dragged in the dirt, stirring up little puffs of dust.

It was a shocking sight. I had become so obsessed with math, I had forgotten what it looked like to see Hana with another girl her age, chatting on the playground. She wasn't teased or actively disliked, just ignored. The weekends had become long stretches of boredom, made even more unbearable because when they were over, she had to go back to school and endure the social wasteland again.

There was no barrage of tests for a social difference. No one I could sue, even if I did have a real lawyer not just a dressed up friend.

If modern science could fix the math issue, if it could fix my graying hair, what else could be fixed? I had been swept up in the disorienting fantasy that good parenting was all about making your child as perfect as possible.

It was time to talk to my dad.

Did I mention that my father is a child psychiatrist?

He and my mother lived just a few blocks away in the tiny ranch house where I'd enjoyed a blissful childhood formed by two things.

First, my parents had intense ideas about privacy. They didn't believe that my business was their business or their business mine. This was based partly on a familial trait of almost phobic shyness. But also, it was influenced by a Freudian notion of the intense issues that exist between parents and children. Oral stages, anal stages, latency, puberty——all this crucial development was to be treated respectfully and carefully. Feelings and thoughts that were invisible and unspoken were the most important, real things in the world. There was a sacred respect for the child's inner world.

A sacred respect for the child's inner world.

The second aspect that shaped my childhood were my two best friends, Sue O'Connor and Amy Weiss.

Sue was fearless, poor, Catholic, tough as nails, and beautiful. She had freckles, a button nose, and divorced parents.

Too cool.

Amy was rich, Jewish, tough as nails, and beautiful. She did things in elementary school that don't happen these days till college, if even then.

My parents let me hang out with these girls without reservation. (Back to the privacy thing.) We ran through the neighborhood, wild and free. My parents rarely called. They never asked what we did, or who was there. It was my life. We could do exactly as we liked without the intervention or hovering of grownups.

They trusted me.

My friends were the ultimate Others. They showed me a way of being that I couldn't ever have imagined existed. This was the gift my parents gave me: the freedom to see all kinds of lives, to dream myself into another person's skin, to imagine the possibilities apart from my family's narrow slice of existence. I learned to see things from different points of view and to be a part of the lives of others without passing judgment.

My daughter was missing this side of life, and it was killing me.

So I asked my father what he thought I should do.

"Nothing."

Now this was irritating.

"She's miserable."

"Really? You sure? She looks okay."

"She has no close friends."

"So? Maybe she's not ready. She'll have them when she's ready."

"That can't be right," I said.

"She's at school six hours a day, surrounded by her peers. Maybe that's enough for her," he suggested. "Sounds exhausting to me."

This wasn't what I had wanted to hear. Remember, I had lost my mind. I was completely convinced that I held the key to my daughter's happiness, both present and future. I was sure that I knew the way to fix anything that needed fixing. And worst of all, I was absolutely sure that she needed fixing.

I was thinking therapy, specifically, the new behavioral therapy aimed at "curing" social anxiety. The idea was that kids who don't interact "correctly" have to be taught to make friends. I had a whole shelf full of books on this subject, some aimed at the parent, others written on a child's level for Hana to read. *The Unspoken Rules of Friendship* was my bible. I left *Jarvis Clutch—Social Spy* on Hana's bedside table.

I should have known my father would think this was all bunk.

Hana did, too, refusing to lift the covers of my literary offerings. "They're stupid," she'd declare, and go back to her fantasy novels.

"I'm going to take her for anxiety therapy," I told my father.

"Sounds like that might create more anxiety. Just let her be. She'll figure it out herself when she's ready," my dad counseled.

Despite the grand memories I had of my childhood, I still didn't trust this gentle man who had raised me.

Psychologists, like lawyers and learning specialists, were big players in our anxious community. Parents slipped me cards of the specialists their child saw. Was every child in therapy? Scratch the surface of this place, and there was a web of misery.

I started Hana at a prestigious Child Anxiety Clinic at a local college, about half an hour from our house. Twice a week, we drove to the campus. I played soccer with Isaiah in the empty playground of a nursery school across the parking lot from the clinic while Hana worked with her psychologist.

The Philadelphia suburbs were as packed with empty playgrounds as they were with therapists.

They gave Hana a workbook called *The Coping Cat*.

"Ooh!" I gushed. "You love cats."

Hana rolled her eyes at me. "Their pictures stink. How is it possible that they made a cat ugly?"

I paid eighty dollars an hour for a young therapist/student to go through *Coping Cat* with Hana. *Coping Cat* was supposed to help kids recognize and understand their emotions. The idea was to show them that their own negative thoughts were all that kept them from happiness. *Coping Cat* offered Hana a four-step plan, summarized by the acronym FEAR.

F for Feeling Frightened.

E for Expecting bad things to happen.

A for Action and Attitude.

R for Results and Rewards.

Hana was asked to think of a situation when she felt scared. *Going to computer lab yesterday,* she wrote. *Walking down the hall.*

What did she expect to happen? *Worrying that I wouldn't be able to do it. To log on or off. It's so confusing.*

What would her coping thoughts be to change her attitude? What Actions and Attitudes could she take that would help? *I can ask for help from the teachers. I can raise my hand. I can think: this is fine.*

And what were the Results and Rewards? *I did good!*

Really?

Hana had come home from school earlier that day, eyes red from crying. "I hate computer lab," she'd told me.

"Don't the teachers help?"

"They're too old," she said. "They don't know how to work the computers any better than I do. They might even be worse, if that's possible."

My father listened to my stories with quiet empathy. "Sometimes," he suggested. "Their fears are real."

Indeed.

"She wants me to color in the pictures of Coping Cat," Hana said one day from the back of the car after a session. "Like I'm five years old. I could draw a cat better than their cat."

This wasn't helping. In fact, it seemed to be having the opposite effect.

Friends confided in me some of the advice their children's therapists gave. One therapist counseled the parents to force their third-grader to call boys to set up play dates every Saturday morning and to keep calling until someone said yes.

I could hear the voice of my father echoing in my head. *Just let Hana be. She'll do what she needs when she's ready. Don't push.*

"I go in," the mother of another child told me, "and tell the therapist what the problem is and he addresses it."

Wait, whose therapy was this? The mother's or the child's? If the mother was allowed to set the agenda, something wasn't right.

But wasn't that exactly what I was doing with Hana? She had never once come to me and said, "I have no close friends and it's lonely and awful." That was my interpretation of her solitary state. Just like with violin, reading, and math, I and the other grownups involved with Hana had an idea of how things should be, our image of the perfect child, and when reality didn't mesh, it made us frantic, panicked, fraught. Or, worse, just plain angry.

"Why does Isaiah get you for an hour while I'm stuck inside with crayons and pictures of a diseased cat?" Hana asked after one session.

Isaiah and I had invented a kind of soccer game where he'd have to hit the huge oak tree in the middle of the playground with the soccer ball to score. I'd try to get the ball from him, or to block his shot. This was more hilarious than an earnest battle, as even at seven years old he was crazy fast, adept at getting around me unless I grabbed at his limbs, which of course I did, leading to epic wrestling-hug fights. It was hard to keep the rosy glow from our play off our faces when Hana emerged from her therapy.

"There's nothing more frightening and dangerous than a clique of nine-year-old girls," another relative told me. She was also a psychiatrist and a former president of the American Psychoanalytic Association. Social fear can make damn good sense, people were trying to tell me. A child's emotions must be respected, not disallowed or manipulated.

We quit the therapy just as we'd quit Suzuki, thousands of dollars poorer and with very little to show for it but a deeper understanding of how pointless it was to try to mold this intelligent, insightful child into the shape I deemed appropriate.

"Did you get anything out of it?" a friend asked.

We had. Hana had set herself to learning how to sketch a proper cat. She was getting pretty darn good at it.

Chapter 14

by Hana: What Did You Do Today—Part II

My mother loves crossword puzzles. I have no idea why. They give me headaches. Every day, she does the *New York Times* crossword puzzle while we eat breakfast. It's super easy on Monday, harder Tuesday and so on.

She stops after Thursday.

"One day, I'll finish a Friday," she insists.

She might because she cheats.

She fills in a few words (probably wrong), then goes to a blog called Rex Parker, King of Crosswords. He's some guy who does the puzzle every day and blogs about it. Then other people come on and argue with him about the most boring stuff you could imagine.

"See, some of them say RBIS is wrong, because RBI means Runs Batted In, so it's already plural. You can't make it more plural," my mother says, scrolling through the hundreds of comments on the blog. "Runs batted ins. It doesn't make sense. Isn't that interesting?"

Life is too short.

So one day, Rex Parker (that's not his real name, just his blog name) tells everyone that he's had his first puzzle accepted in the *Times*. He's now officially a constructor. It'll come out the next week.

This is a big deal for him.

He asks his blog readers to do his puzzle and then send their completed puzzles to him to mark the day.

"But we just do it in pencil," Isaiah says. "He won't want ours since it's not in pen." There had been a long discussion a while back in the comments about how a lot of Rex's loyal followers do the puzzle in pen.

"Sure he will. He doesn't care how we do it," my mother says.

"Well, I think we should do it in pen," Isaiah says.

Isaiah cares what an old guy with a made up name thinks. I have no idea why.

"We could do it in pencil, then write over it in pen," my mother suggests.

Isaiah doesn't like this idea. "We have to do it in pen."

She's doubtful. It's a Tuesday puzzle, so not super-hard. But not the easiest either.

"I could do it in embroidery," I say.

They both stare at me.

"Really?" my mother says.

"Sure. I've got white felt. Black floss." I look over the puzzle. A grid, fifteen by fifteen. "It would take me one soccer practice, maybe two."

"Would you do that?" she asks. She's really excited. She loves Rex like I love Doe Deere, my favorite blogger, so I understand. I'd do anything for Doe Deere.

They do the puzzle in pencil. I take their answers and trace them onto the felt. Embroider it. The D's and R's are hard, but the rest of it goes pretty quick.

We send it to Rex and hear nothing.

For weeks.

"I guess he just isn't the politest guy," my mother says. "But I'm sure he appreciated it. Some people just don't have manners."

Months go by.

We forget about it.

My mom still goes to his blog Monday through Thursday, but I think she's even a little pissed at him. That thing was pretty cool.

Then, one day in November, four months after his puzzle was published, we get a thank you letter in the mail from Rex. My mom figures our package must have gotten lost for a while in the mail. He wrote that he blogged about my puzzle last Saturday, but since the Saturday puzzle is so hard, my mom doesn't even cheat at it. We missed his blog about our puzzle.

This is what Rex had written on his blog:

> "Dear Diana, Isaiah, and *especially* Hana, I got your package today, and I don't really know what to say except — I'm incredibly touched, and incredibly grateful (see hand-stitched rendering of my NYT xword debut, below). One of the nicest things anyone (who doesn't know me personally) has ever done for me. I mean ... I showed my wife and *she* teared up. The grid, along with your note with the (aDORable) pictures, will hang on my wall forever. Seriously awesome. As one of my Facebook friends said when I posted the pic to my FB wall: "That's up there with Van Gogh's ear as far as impressive presents go."

I disagree with that.

Sending an ear to someone is disgusting. My puzzle, on the other hand, rocked.

Chapter 15

by Diana: Fifth Grade

All the research about education points to one simple fact: Good teachers can teach. Bad ones can't.

In fifth grade, our second year in Philadelphia, Hana was lucky enough to get an excellent teacher.

This brilliant woman along with Hana's stellar extra-help math teacher lifted the veil of anxiety that had hung over Hana for her first year in the suburbs.

After her year in the wilderness, she started to make good friends.

By October, she had a best friend, Patty Stern.

Patty was a "creative" kid, too (as if there are uncreative kids), who liked to sew and draw. Hana was pulled on Patty's coattails into her group of girls who had been friends since kindergarten.

Oh, the sweet, sweet relief of a mother who knows her kid has someone to sit with at lunch.

All our problems had been solved by time and patience. They had turned out to be momentary blips on the upward trajectory of my brilliant daughter.

Fifth grade rushed by in a whirl of friends and academic success.

Sure, I knew that middle school was on the horizon.

That alone should have been enough to strike fear into my heart.

Middle school.

Puberty.

But things were good. I had obviously figured it all out. What a mother I was! A little intense, but a good balance. I was a tamed tiger who was starting to understand that I couldn't micromanage everything, that the hard times would pass, that life was going to be okay even if it had its ups and downs which were best handled with grace and patience, rather than panic and force.

What could possibly go wrong?

PART II: *Middle School*

"Far better to live your own path imperfectly
than to live another's perfectly."

—Bhagavad-Gita

Chapter 16

by Diana: Happy Birthday to Hana

Sixth grade was hell.

Sheer, utter, endless hell.

And I didn't have to set foot in school. How must it have been for Hana, who had to actually show up every day and stay for hours?

Patty dropped Hana from her friend roster like a leper. It took a few months for this to sink in. At our annual Halloween party, I caught Patty and another girl whispering furtively on the stairs. They giggled, their eyes on Hana.

My heart iced over.

Maybe I was being too sensitive. Maybe I had it wrong.

I didn't.

The next night, the girls were going trick-or-treating. Hana had spent hours sewing her colonial girl costume, and didn't want to join the pack.

"I hate big groups," she said. "No one will be able to see my costume."

I couldn't endure the humiliation of her trick-or-treating alone. "It's not so big."

"I don't want to go with them," she insisted.

"You're going. They invited you. It'll be fun." Yes, I still hit that frail, pathetic word a little too hard. Six years after Suzuki, and I'd learned nothing.

Patty's father, a few other parents, and I tagged after the pack of kids. After the night was over, Hana and I walked home, exhausted. My face was flushed with success. So good to be back in the swing.

"I hated that," she told me.

"You looked like you were having fun," I said.

"I wasn't," she insisted. "Jane was so bossy. She kept making us go back to her house because she wanted water or to rest or to pet her dog or whatever. Why does everyone do what she says? I don't get it. And Melanie was so slow. I wanted to kill her. And no one saw my costume. I was always pushed to the back."

"Costumes and candy aren't really the point of Halloween," I pointed out.

She rolled her eyes at me. To Hana, costumes and candy were exactly the point. "I'm not going with them next year. I'm making a great costume and going by myself so that people can see it."

I will die of sadness, I thought. *I cannot endure that.*

I should have seen Hana's independence and celebrated it. But I couldn't. I still wanted her to fit in. I so badly didn't want her to be the kid walking alone, house to house, missing what I deemed the point of Halloween, that I didn't care a whit about what she wanted.

A month or so later, the last time Patty was in the back of our car, I overheard the girls discussing Jane, the bossy girl with the dog and the need for constant, entourage-accompanied rest stops.

"Why don't you like her?" Patty asked.

"Do you really like her?" Hana asked, incredulous.

"No. Not really. But her dad has season tickets to the Phillies. If you're nice to her, you get to go. You sit right behind home plate."

As I steered my ancient Subaru onto Patty's street, I couldn't help thinking that Patty understood something fundamental that Hana failed to grasp. Sure, I knew it was awful to use people as means to an end. Yet I still admired Patty's ability to see the obvious: in middle school, it's not whom you like, it's who gets you where you want to go. Who has the Phillies tickets, the connections, the fun.

We dropped Patty off in front of her beautiful, perfectly-tended house, her lawn pristine with every blade of grass the proper color and height. Her parent's brand new Range Rover glistened in the driveway.

"Bye, Pat," Hana called.

But Patty didn't answer. She slammed the door without looking back.

She'd never grace the back of our car again.

#

Patty broke off from the group to pursue her own social life. Hana, who disliked all groups, had only existed in Patty's clique by association.

Hana was left hanging.

Every day, at three-twenty-two, I'd hear her come through the back door alone, and my heart would sink. I'd put on my happy-fun-face and greet her, then go back to work upstairs, listening to the sounds of my daughter and her new best friend, the television.

I'd wait till nighttime to cry.

Other mothers would kindly regale me with stories of Patty's moral and academic failings. The missteps of this go-getter twelve-year-old helped ease the pain, but just a little.

Despite that I'd just recently witnessed Hana's fourth grade/fifth grade transformation, this lonely state seemed like the way it would be forever.

Hana drifted through the year. I'd encourage her to call the girls whose names she'd mention from her classes. "How about Kelly? What about Remy?" But she'd scoff at me as if I understood nothing.

Of course, she was right. I didn't. The middle school social landscape was complex and nuanced.

When it was time for her birthday party in January, I was filled with dread. Couldn't we just skip this painful rite of passage?

No way. Hana wanted a party.

"How about bowling?" I suggested.

"You can't be serious."

She knew exactly what she wanted to do.

My husband had an apartment in Princeton that year. He was on sabbatical at the Institute for Advanced Studies there and had to retain a residence, even though it was just over an hour from our house. He'd drive up to Princeton on Monday and stay through Thursday, getting work done on his book while he hobnobbed with the other Institute scholars over cookies and tea in the Einstein Drawing Room. The apartment was small and spartan, grad student style living, but it had a fireplace in which to toast marshmallows.

Just outside the Institute was a small pond. When it froze over, they put up a green flag to indicate it was safe to skate on.

Hana wanted to take some friends to Princeton, skate on the

pond, toast marshmallows in the fireplace, and have a sleepover in the apartment.

My stomach hurt just thinking about this.

"Only two friends," I told her. "I can't fit anymore in the car."

Could we find two girls to come?

The most likely contender had soccer games every weekend, it seemed, until she was twenty-one. The next one, a shy, quiet girl said yes. But Hana and one friend didn't seem enough for a party. We went through a list of possible kids. Finally, Hana chose a girl I knew nothing about.

She said yes also.

This, of course, should have calmed me. It should have clued me in to the fact that Hana wasn't alone: lots of kids were drifting in social uncertainty. It was, after all, middle school. Plus, it showed that Hana wasn't disliked; she was just outside the circle. But it was hard to keep the big picture in mind when I was so maniacally focused on my own child.

We somehow managed to beg and borrow the correct size skates for everyone. We bought marshmallows. We planned where and what to eat, gathered enough bedding, and packed the car. The weather had been in the low twenties for weeks. We couldn't assure it for the day of her party, but the green flag had been up on Thursday, when my husband had left town.

Still, I wasn't entirely sure I could go through with this. There are very few times in my life that I understand why people drink alcohol. This was one of them. Yet I couldn't drink a drop, as I was the designated driver.

The car ride was mostly silent, with me trying lamely to stimulate conversation or pretending that it was natural to have three silent girls in my car for over an hour.

When we got to Princeton, the flag was red. No skating allowed.

I wanted to throw up.

Hana's face crumbled.

Now what? It was twenty degrees and we were an hour from home with hours and hours stretching out in front of us till dinnertime.

Why couldn't Hana have just had a bowling party like everyone else? I wanted a normal kid with normal birthday parties—inside, scheduled, tested, guaranteed.

Then the girls realized that the pond was surrounded by vast frozen puddles.

"Can we skate on those?"

Why not?

They laced up their skates and tentatively tried the puddles.

The puddles linked to a network of trails. The trails led to the woods.

All the trails were frozen over with a layer of smooth, sparkling ice.

The girls' faces lit up with joy.

They whizzed through the beautiful Institute woods, whooping and singing. They grinned, enchanted by the magic of their personal ice skating rink under the treetops.

They fell. They pulled each other up. They fell again. Their breath puffed in little clouds before them as they panted on logs until they were ready to fly off again.

I followed gamely, skittering along in my boots.

We came to a quaint bridge over an even quainter stream.

"Oh my God, this is so fun!" the girls exclaimed.

They took off their skates and put on their boots and played in the icy steam till their fingers were white with cold. Then, exhausted, we trudged the mile or so back to the apartment, our breath puffing in happy clouds.

We had dinner at a little Indian restaurant, but the food was too weird for them. One girl ate only bread. The other carefully nibbled at the corner of a pakora. Conversation over dinner was awkward.

I checked and rechecked my watch.

I set the GPS and took the girls to a terrible movie the next town over.

On the way back, just before midnight, the GPS steered us onto an access road into a forest.

The ground was icy and rutted. It was pitch dark. My two headlights were the only source of eerie light in the rapidly descending fog. I was terrified. Everything had started out so well, but now we'd die of exposure in the wilderness.

Or, worse, we'd live.

I imagined us shivering in the freezing dark, waiting for AAA to pull us out, every minute melting another tenuous bond that Hana had so carefully formed with these little girls. Hana's link to them still felt as delicate as the icicles hanging off the enormous pines that towered over us.

I threw the car in reverse, cursed like a sailor, and propelled us out of the ice and snow.

Thank God for my Subaru.

The next fourteen hours and thirty-seven minutes passed slowly.

By breakfast the next morning, I couldn't wait to get out of there. I felt like an athlete on my last lap, racing for the finish line. If I could only get them home alive and unbroken, then I'd have an entire year until next year's birthday party.

What was wrong with me? That party had been magical. Surely, they'd never forget the sensation of flying through the forest on skates. Chances were these girls would never, ever do anything like it again in their lives.

It was as unique a moment as discovering the sea of hats under the bridge.

As unique as the intricate, homemade Halloween costumes Hana sewed every year.

Or the embroidered crossword puzzle a complete stranger hung on his wall.

As unique as her unwillingness to ever, ever even consider a bowling party.

Or her refusal be friends with the girl with Phillies tickets just because.

So why was I still the mother who wished her kid would be like everyone else? As I drove the girls home, I meditated on the rift between what I wanted Hana to be and what she was. Hana possessed stunning originality, a complete lack of caring what anyone thought, an unwillingness to back down in the face of what would knock other kids flat.

What had happened in those woods wasn't magic; it was Hana.

She just wanted to fly through the forest, and she didn't give a crap if anyone followed or not.

That concern was my problem.

When it came to this child, I was still missing the point.

Chapter 17

by Hana: What I Wore—Part I

Middle school made me crazy because everyone dressed exactly the same. I get why they did it, but I didn't like it. I think clothes are important. They let other people know a little about who you are.

But part of wearing what I want has nothing to do with anyone else. It's about fun. It's fun to wear bows and bright colors and unicorn prints. It makes me happy. What you do should make you happy, and part of what you do is get dressed every day.

Also, with people like me who don't talk a lot, clothes say what you would say if the people who are so loud would ever stop talking. But those people never stop talking. So with clothes, I can say what I want and I don't have to worry about all the shouting around me.

I hate shouting.

Dressing the way I wanted didn't start all at once. It took time to develop a style. My style is whimsical. I love stuff that's beautiful and colorful and fun.

For instance, these earrings were some of the first I made myself.

I had just learned how to crochet and had so many crocheted balls. I tried to make earrings out of the biggest ones but they were too heavy. So I decided to take the smallest ones and made earrings out of them. I love how they turned out.

I still love my ball earrings, but they were a first step. That's fun sometimes. But other times, you want something a little more magical. It took about a year to get from my ball earrings to these:

These earrings are a foam ball cut in half with some gold and silver trim hot glue gunned around them. The trim is from a box full of reenactor scraps that we bought for five dollars at a garage sale. Reenactors, if you don't know, are people who like to dress up like old fashioned soldiers and pretend. They make their own costumes, and the trim is incredible. We were super lucky to get all this.

Anyway, on the top I hot glue gunned some fake flowers and attached a chain. I really like big statement earrings. I think that these look like two fancy octopuses.

I love this bow headband.

I love the fabric with the cherries on it. I was at the fabric store to pick out fabric for two things, a skirt and a bag. I wanted to make the skirt out of the cherries but my friend and mom talked me out of it. But I got the cherry fabric for the bag, and with the extra fabric I made this headband.

Even though I love my cherry bow, I love this bow more.

A lot of bows are too tiny. This one is giant and gets your attention. Instead of looking at my eyes, people talk to the bow. It's funny to watch.

When I made this bow, it broke the sewing machine needle because the fabric got really thick.

It was worth it.

After I made it, I attached it to a headband. It's one of my favorite things to wear to school because it's so normal to wear a bow in your hair.

Just not this one.

Chapter 18

by Diana: Boys, Bat Mitzvahs, & Boxing

I will keep my anxieties to myself.

I will get the heck out of Hana's way.

Home will be a place of safety and comfort absolutely and completely. A haven. When the door clicks closed behind Hana, she will sigh in relief. She will not have to steel herself to fight me off.

This was my new mantra, but it wasn't easy. I wanted to barrage her with questions the minute she walked in the door about who she ate lunch with (a group of girls who barely seemed to speak). I was desperate to tease out of her who she did projects with (whoever was left over, usually one of the kids with a one-on-one aide). I wanted to scream at her in desperation, "Do you open your mouth in school at all? Even once?" (That would usually elicit a shrug and, "Not really. Why?")

But no more of that.

If she wanted to come home every day alone, that was fine. I was going to act on my values of honoring her inner life and accepting that she might not fit in, but who cared? In fact, hooray for her.

All this noninvolvement took work.

She'd flop in front of the television or computer and my insides would boil. *Get out there and do something,* I was desperate to shout at her, preferably while poking her with a sharp stick.

No, no, I'd scold myself. *She's been out of the house, dealing all day with middle school. She deserves to rest without her psychotic mother hounding her. Just lay off and let her be.* I had to constantly remind myself that I was the one who sat at home alone all day in front of my computer, not her.

But I couldn't let up.

Physical fitness, you understand, was a worthy endeavor. Nothing wrong with badgering a child over that. Studies proved it. This wasn't her over-anxious mother talking. This was science.

"You must chose a sport," I told her.

"Okay. I want to row crew," she said after some thought.

No go. You had to be five-foot-two to row crew. She was at least five inches too short. Plus, she didn't weigh more than eighty pounds.

"I want to rock climb," she said.

The nearest rock climbing wall in downtown Philadelphia had a tricky, alternate weekend-only schedule for kids. The next closest wall was forty minutes away without traffic.

There was always traffic. Bad traffic.

By this point, I was driving Isaiah insane distances a couple of times a week to practice soccer. But that felt different. He was steadily climbing up the ranks of elite soccer players, and he took his sport seriously. It was his team, his passion, his life, while rock climbing was an untested whim—and an expensive one at that.

"I want to box," Hana said.

"Hit people?" I asked, horrified. But I quickly gathered myself, the Zen mother. "Okay, how about Taekwondo?" I had earned my yellow belt years ago in a dingy fifth floor studio in New York City, so I knew a little about it.

"No. Boxing."

"What's the difference between boxing and Taekwondo?"

"No way am I putting on one of those ugly white get-ups."

It was a fashion issue.

"I bet we could find a martial arts place that doesn't make you wear the uniforms," I told her, not the least bit sure at all.

"But why? What's the difference between Taekwondo and boxing? I'd rather just box than do all that stupid screaming. I don't like to scream."

What was the difference? Well, that was easy. Little blonde girls from the Main Line didn't go into sweaty South Philly boxing gyms with the express goal of hitting people. They did more seemly, intellectual fighting, where success was measured by the color of your belt, not the maiming of your opponent.

Karate would be okay.

Tae Bo, fine.

I had no idea what Tae Bo was, but you get the idea. I didn't know much about this stuff, but I knew where I stood.

"You're such a hypocrite," Hana said. "You said I could pick any sport, but every sport I pick, you shoot down. I won't keep picking until just soccer is left. I'm not chasing a stupid ball around a field with a bunch of girls in ponytails and elastic headbands."

As usual, she had a point.

So boxing it was.

We met Joey, a Jesus-tattooed Manayunk native with a store-front gym on Main Street. A picture of his mom airbrushed onto the back of a sweatshirt dominated the front window display. Later, he'd tell us that when he got in trouble in school, his mom used to show up and literally try to beat him up in the hallway. "She had a mean left hook."

Now that was a tiger mother.

His studio was just over the bridge from where we lived.

Over the bridge was another world.

"C'mon, girl!" he'd bellow in his husky, Rocky Balboa voice. "Hit it! Right, left, right jab. Go!" He'd dance backward, huge mitts covering his own huge mitts, while Hana wailed on him. "That's a girl! C'mon! Harder!"

Hana loved boxing. If she missed too many sessions, she'd say, "I really feel like hitting someone."

I'd drop her off two afternoons a week. While I'd run on the Schuylkill River Trail or sit in La Colombe and sip excellent coffee that would keep me up all night, Hana would bind her hands in long, black Mexican hand wraps and wail on the heavy bags, or deftly tap, tap, tap at the timing bags. When she'd spar with other boxers, I couldn't watch.

She loved every minute of it.

Joey was a classic.

When he posed naked for the *Philadelphia Magazine* Best Bodies issue and put the framed article in his front window next to his Mom sweatshirt, I had a moment of doubt. Was this really an appropriate place for a thirteen-year-old girl to hang out?

But Hana was a supremely appropriate thirteen-year-old girl. She didn't seem into boys at all, much less a forty-three-year-old boxer with a diamond stud embedded in his chin.

"You know, the muscle grows around it," Hana told me gleefully. "It becomes part of his face."

And so she boxed.

When she wasn't at school, or boxing, or watching Tyra Banks break some six-foot-something, doe-eyed girl's heart on *America's Next Top Model*, she sometimes could be found at a bat mitzvah. This was, after all, seventh grade in a predominantly Jewish suburb. Everyone got a few invites, no matter how disconnected they were from the social scene.

It wasn't unusual for a bat mitzvah on the Main Line to cost over thirty-thousand dollars. Parents would plan lavish parties with five-piece bands, sit-down dinners, dessert bars with chocolate fondue fountains, photo booths, entertainers, party "poppers" (post-pubescent dancers paid to stir the pre-pubescent crowd into a frenzy), and take-home party favors—usually custom-designed sweatshirts.

The Monday after the parties, everyone would wear their "I Went to Josie's Bat Mitzvah" sweatshirts to school.

One night at dinner, Hana said, "Nora's bat mitzvah is this weekend and every girl in my English class is going but me."

"That sucks," I said, trying to hold my heart in my throat.

"They'll all come to school on Monday and wear their I-went-to-Nora's-Bat-Mitzvah sweatshirts."

"That doesn't seem very nice," I said, trying not to call Nora's mother right then and there to berate her for her insensitivity. But the sweatshirt thing was ubiquitous. It wasn't Nora's fault or her mother's. It was part of the culture—which says just about everything you need to know about the culture.

"I don't care. It's so stupid. They look like little clones," she said.

I could tell there was something on her mind. Poor kid, I thought. She does care. Of course she cares. How hurtful. I could have ripped up all their shirts in a whirlwind of righteous anger.

While I searched for words, she went on carefully. "So I was thinking. Could we go out this weekend and buy a sweatshirt and I'll write on it, *I Didn't Go to Nora's Bat Mitzvah*. I already know her colors are hot pink and blue. I could make it look really, really great."

Oh. My. God.

"Really? You'd do that?" I managed to get out. Why did I always get Hana so wrong? She wasn't being depressed; she was making a plan. How did it feel to be this amazingly brave, defiant girl? I had no idea, because I was a big old wimp.

"Sure, why not?" she asked.

If she pulled it off, it wouldn't just be hilarious and daring. It would be art. It would be the most brilliant piece of performance art that that middle school had ever seen. Possibly any middle school.

Pride stirred inside me. It felt a little like the pride I'd felt carrying her tiny violin to Suzuki, but it was different in a way that was hard to define. This pride wasn't about an achievement, it was about who she was. I was proud of my child's character, not her accomplishment.

Still, I wasn't there yet. I couldn't let my daughter expose herself in that jungle.

She was ready, but I was still a coward.

"Don't," I cautioned.

"Why not? It would be so cool."

"Please don't," I added.

So she didn't. But only because I wouldn't take her out to buy the sweatshirt. But boy did she want to.

Little did I know, I was just holding off the inevitable.

#

Like I said, she did get invited to a few bat and bar mitzvahs. Because there were so many of them, this meant about one a month.

One Saturday night, I went to pick her up from a bat mitzvah that was taking place on the top floor of a swanky downtown hotel. As was the custom, I parked my car in one of the valet spots outside the hotel's garage and begged the parking guys to let me just run in and collect my daughter and her friends. A five-dollar tip usually did the trick.

I went into the hotel through the dark, tunnel-like garage.

On a bench sat five prostitutes. Their skirts were barely there, their tops even less so, low cut and see-through. They were caked in garish make up, huddled together, trying to keep warm in the wee hours of the cold, Philadelphia night.

Oh my God! Whores! At Joanne's bat mitzvah! Maybe I could take Hana out the front door and around the side.

And then I saw a mother I knew, paying to get her car out of the garage.

I looked more closely at the girls.

Yep, those were kids from the bat mitzvah. Not prostitutes, but twelve-year-old bat mitzvah guests in three-inch heels and teeny dresses, waiting to be chauffeured home by a mom in the spotless

Mercedes.

My bad.

How could I have been worried about what Hana wore? Hana might look odd next to these girls in her homemade dress, but she was escaping the middle school trap that these girls fell into one-by-one: the hyper-sexualization of their still-tiny bodies. I was concerned for her not fitting in, but did I really want her to fit in? What did fitting in mean?

I started to hear disturbing rumors.

"You know what the boys get as a gift at their bar mitzvahs?"

"Kiddush cups?" I asked hopefully.

"A blow job from their guest of choice, under the tables."

Just about every girl in the seventh grade had braces. Didn't that hurt?

Suddenly, I was looking at the girls without braces with concern. *Oh, Sally's going to Stuart's bar mitzvah this weekend? Are you sure that's a good idea?*

A girl in Hana's English class was suspended for sending a boy a picture of her bare breasts. Naturally, the picture had gone viral. The boys who forwarded the picture were given detentions. Later that year, I chaperoned backstage at the school play. The breast-flashing girl and her friends spent their downtime posing with each other lasciviously for the boys, who snapped away delightedly with their cell phones like paparazzi.

Honey, I wanted to tell the girls, *lesbian porno shots really aren't the way to make friends.*

Except, I was wrong. Lesbian porno shots were exactly the way to make friends and these girls knew it.

Hana was alone in the hallway, knitting.

So, she spent her afternoons hitting a guy named Joey covered in Jesus tattoos? In the scheme of things, this was a wholesome pursuit. To fit into a screwed up world, you had to accept the status quo.

Instead, she was fighting actively against it, with and without her fists.

Chapter 19

by Hana: The Next Level

Everyone always tries to fit in. I do the opposite. I want to stand out. I don't want to be like everyone else. It's not to get attention. It's more about taking it to the next level.

What do I mean by that? Well, here are a few examples: I could have worn a tutu to school, but instead I wore two tutus. Or, I could have gone out for after school field hockey like everyone else, but instead, I box twice a week. I could have sewed the panda bear they had in the instruction book, but instead, I made a pandacorn (part panda, part unicorn). Some people think I do things differently because I want attention. But it's not true. I only want to take things further. I want to go to the next level. That's where everything starts to get fun. That's where you get the thrill. Heart pumping, blood flowing, who knows what will happen next?

Throw yourself into the unknown. Don't do what's expected. Think about what you can do, and then do it a little wilder, a little better, a little crazier.

#

Every year at school, they have Spirit Week. Each day has a theme, and you dress up to show your school spirit. I don't have much school spirit, but I like dressing up, so spirit week is my kind of thing.

Monday was dress up as your favorite movie star. I have a lot of favorite movie stars, but none who would be fun to dress up as, so I chose Mephistopheles from *Cats*. I did all the makeup myself and made the ears and the shirt. I think I freaked my real cat out, though.

I won.

Tuesday was Twin Day. My friend Jen and I won it together, even though we look nothing alike.

Wednesday was Fan Day. You were supposed to dress up as a Phillies fan or an Eagles fan.

Could these people be more boring?

I dressed up to support Team Unicorn. I wore sparkly face-paint and feathered fake eyelashes and had a big sign that said, Go Team Unicorn. Everyone loved it.

And yes, I won.

Thursday was Pajama Day. I was the only one in footie long johns. I love footie long johns because they're so cozy. Especially in science class.

Yup. Won it.

Friday was School Colors Day. I don't own any school spirit stuff, since I think it's a waste of money and I don't really like our school's colors—gray and purple. Really? Why? But by the last day, people so much wanted me to sweep the awards, they lent me everything they could. I won wearing everyone else's clothes. It was a group win. That was the funnest day.

Chapter 20

by Diana: Streams of Consciousness

I have a childhood memory that stands out above all other memories as one of pure wonder and joy. One evening, I came home from middle school starving after softball practice. My mother had heated up a batch of frozen french fries for dinner.

To my twelve-year-old self, they smelled sublime.

She divided them into four servings, but after I scarfed mine, I wanted more.

She gave me hers. Just like that. Pushed them onto my plate.

I remember her act of giving me those french fries as a shocking expression of pure generosity. How could she give up something so wonderful with so little thought? How could she give me such happiness? *This was what it meant to be a good person in the world.*

As a parent, that moment floats into my consciousness often. *Give everything, always, selflessly because that is what creates happiness.*

The french fries on a Wednesday evening had become a guiding precept of my life.

Of course, when I look back on that moment, I see that my mother probably didn't like frozen french fries. If she had been anything similar to how I am as a mother, she'd most likely spent the afternoon snacking on Oreos, was stuffed, and feeling too woozy for oily, reheated starch. I'm absolutely certain that if you asked my mother what she did to raise a successful, mentally balanced, kindhearted, happy daughter, she'd probably shrug and say all the usual things—piano lessons, nine-o'clock bedtimes, good oral hygiene.

She wouldn't mention the french fries.

It's a terrifying fact of parenting: we have no idea which moments stick, and which go by. We can't choose the moments that our kids will internalize. So how do we act?

I was faced with this conundrum as I began to feel more and more incompetent as a mother to Hana. All my doing seemed to be going wrong—the Suzuki, the reading, the math, the therapist, the praying for normalcy. Yet, Hana was triumphing in extraordinary, unexpected ways. Why? What was I doing *right*?

Other mothers were investing time and energy in tutors, teachers, therapists, and coaches. I must have had an alternate strategy for raising fearless, independent, successful, children. Because Lord knows, despite it all, that's what Hana was turning out to be. Isaiah, in a completely different way, was also turning out happy, accomplished, generous, and kind.

If I looked closely, could I find my french fry moments?

#

There was an abandoned railroad track behind our house that the township was making into a recreational trail. For years we'd walk along the undeveloped tracks, a narrow, rocky path framed by cliffs of overgrown weeds. Foxes, hawks, armies of rabbits, and lone stray cats with glowing yellow eyes peering out from the undergrowth watched our comings and goings suspiciously.

Hardly any humans saw us, since there was never anyone else there.

A stream flowed off to one side of the trail. But twenty feet of old tires, trash, weeds, and poison ivy between the trail and the stream made reaching it impossible. We'd hear the water trickling, hear the birds frolicking, and think, gee, too bad we can't get to it.

Every so often, Hana and I would join the Friends of the Trail for clean-up days. We'd pick up trash or rip evil mile-a-minute vines from the trees struggling under their oppressive weight. It was surprisingly fun. We'd help plant native trees, move debris, water plantings. Slowly, month by month, The Friends got closer to the stream. We could see the birds now when they rose into the vine-free trees.

Then the township brought in the heavy equipment. Earth movers cut huge swaths through the undergrowth. The detritus of years of neglect was cleared in matter of hours.

The next Sunday afternoon, Hana, my father, and I hiked down the trail. The stream was bigger and wider than I'd expected. Beautiful hundred-year-old stone bridges crossed it here and there as it meandered in lazy, sweeping curves. My father and I sat in the shade on the wall of a bridge watching Hana explore the water below.

I was delighted with our new playground. To have natural beauty so close at hand reminded me of Ithaca. Hana was back in the world she'd known as a child. When she grew tired of the hopping rock to rock, she climbed to the top of a two-story heap of downed trees, their limbs already bleaching white in the sun. Eventually, Hana skipped back to the stream, sending a flock of robins into the trees. After a bit, she cried, "I can't wait to bring my friends here."

She asked everyone she could think of to come with her to the stream.

I overheard one boy ask, "We're going to play in a stream?" as if she'd proposed they go hot-wire the neighbor's Mercedes and take it for a joy ride.

Concerned parents called to ask me to explain the concept. "Is it safe?" they'd ask.

"Just check after for ticks," I'd say happily.

I'd never hear from those parents again.

A few of her friends agreed to go, but they wore strappy sandals and had trouble on the rocks. One dropped her cell phone into the water and it took Hana and her brother half an hour to fish it out.

As the weeks and months went by it became clear that although hundreds of children lived within a half mile of the stream, none save Hana cared that it existed. I suppose they were inside playing video games or watching TV. Some were undoubtedly doing what seemed to be all the rage these days, crank phone calling less popular kids. Most kids, though, were at one Very Important scheduled event or another, learning crucial skills that would (hopefully) get them into Harvard.

Why was Hana the only one outside? I remembered Hana's Waldorf teacher, Sue, who used to celebrate the first frost with a joyful march of three and four year olds to the waterfall to see the ice, to play in it, to marvel over its beauty. In the summertime, Sue would walk those same twelve pre-schoolers over a mile to the swimming hole, then back again after a day spent frolicking in the water. She taught them how to see the birds, to notice the trees, and know which berries to eat.

In Hana's public school in Ithaca, they'd go out in any weather, even in upstate New York's frigid winters. "There's no bad weather, just bad clothing," the teachers would say.

Here, they'd have indoor recess if the ground was wet. Or if there were too many leaves on the playground. *Much too slippery*, they'd say as they cancelled outdoor recess for most of October. The kids sat in heated seats in idling cars to wait for the school bus because concerned mothers didn't want their little ones out in the cold. We lived less than half a mile from the school, but the mothers on our block organized a carpool because walking was too cold, wet, and unsafe.

Learning to appreciate nature, like learning to read, to play an instrument, or to do times tables took work. It took time. It took resources. A parent had to start early, be diligent and disciplined.

Handwork was another skill deemed important and worthwhile in Ithaca. When we moved, Hana had insisted I not throw out any of her countless boxes of crafting materials. To add to the chaos, I had a relative who kept an entire apartment in the Bronx stuffed with fabric and other notions. When she passed away, Hana inherited hundreds of wooden spools of thread, ancient buttons, snaps, fabric, zippers, beads, and sequins. Hana's room became a toppling, complicated tangle of yarn, thread, fabric, wool, and other art supplies. Every scrap was too precious to throw out. Other mothers would see her collections upon collections, like cities scattered across the uncertain landscape of her room, and gasp in horror at the mess. Her room was legendary.

But I understood the magic of that room. I'd find Hana on her bed late at night, embroidering complicated stitches from a book I'd gotten her years ago but she'd never bothered to look at until now. Good thing she had all that embroidery thread from 1967 stashed in a drawer along with seven nickel packs of needles from Woolworth's in every shape and size. If this child got an urge to decorate her Converse sneakers, or recreate a shirt she'd seen at a store for too much money to buy, or copy a *New Yorker* magazine cover that she adored, she could do it without adult permission or interference.

This kid could work her sewing machine with the skill and panache of a musician. She could put in a zipper, set a buttonhole, hem a skirt, set a sleeve, even fix the machine when it broke down.

"What are you doing?" I'd ask, finding her one day in the center of a pile of wool and whatnot.

"Needle felting," she'd say, holding up a tiny, exquisite baby bird made of wool. How the heck did she know how to do that? I'd forgotten the needles, the wool, the beautiful instruction book she'd found at that garage sale years ago. But she remembered, and when she was ready, she somehow knew where her supplies were in that astonishing mess. She could pick a project up and work at it until she was on to the next thing that caught her interest.

Turns out that all the time we'd spent "doing nothing" in Ithaca had actually been remarkably productive. All those days spent playing outside had sculpted a fit, healthy body on a child who loved nature with passion. All those hours in the wilds of our insanely huge sandbox had molded a kid with the creativity to make whatever she wanted from whatever was at hand. All those evenings in front of the fire knitting endless scarves had shaped a child with the exceptional hand control to manage whatever task she set out on.

We hadn't noticed that we were doing any of these things at the time because there were no awards for being a three-year-old who could joyfully hike a mile in February in upstate New York. There was no elite team of knitters run by parents who didn't let the other children join in because the knitting squad was too advanced for lesser talents who couldn't cast off at high speeds in the European method. There were no prestigious teachers of outdoor exploration who auditioned a select few, rejecting the ones who couldn't retrieve a cell phone with a stick while balancing over a leafy stream.

Conventional, boring, uptight society didn't value the skills she was developing; didn't reward them; didn't even notice them. But the gorgeous thing was, it didn't matter. She was doing what she was doing for the pure joy of doing it. The doing was its own reward, because she hadn't been taught to crave recognition and reward.

I had finally uncovered an essential truth about parenting that I could live by. Something concrete to hold on to. Tiger mothers were wrong: it was easy to be a bully, to yell, scream, and scare your children into doing what you wanted them to do and then bask in society's accolades. The hard path was to let children find their own bliss, even if it might never lead to societal recognition. Detached, emotionally-neutral, patient parenting was a slow, gradual process. In fact, the process was so slow and so gradual, a parent might miss it if they weren't aware.

This was the joy of the rebel—not caring what anyone thought, but acting out of pure passion and love. This was the joy of living an examined, respectful life where feelings and thoughts mattered—harmony. No yelling. No stress. Doing what you love for the pure joy of it.

I could have gotten out the flashcards, insisted on the Suzuki, pushed at the therapy. But instead, I'd let Hana be a child and taught her that what mattered was kindness, thoughtfulness, respect, and beauty.

I'd also taught her, by my happy Ithaca years being a failure at writing, that there was nothing wrong with failing. Who cared what the world thought if you were getting closer to something so worthwhile? Fail, be rejected, but never stop. Keep on pushing. It's the only way to be.

I had been giving away my french fries one by one, and just like my mother before me, I hadn't even known I was doing it.

Chapter 21

by Hana: What Did You Do Today—Part II

I was walking home from school behind two sixth graders. I recognized one of them as a kid who sometimes hung out with my brother.

They were harassing a girl walking in front of them who was minding her own business. She looked like she was in their grade, but I didn't know her.

"What's your favorite color?" they asked.

"Shut up," she said.

"Just tell us your favorite color." They were saying it in a way that let you know it was some kind of disgusting joke.

She tried to ignore them, but they wouldn't stop.

Finally, I couldn't take it anymore. "Leave her alone. You're disgusting."

They whirled around.

They'd been ignoring me.

Smart boys.

Now, they were surprised and a little nervous. "It's not your business," the taller one said.

The smaller one was just the tagalong, so I ignored him. There was always a tagalong with these kind of kids. The wimpy follower who wanted so badly to belong.

"It is my business. Because you're bugging a girl in a way that bothers her and so it bothers me. You can't talk to girls like that. You think it's cool, but it's not." I had just finished reading *Cinderella Ate My Daughter: Dispatches from the Frontlines of the New Girlie-Girl Culture*. One point of the book was that you have to control how other people see you. I agreed with that completely. It was up to you. You had the power. Those boys were trying to take her power. She didn't know how to hold onto her power.

The boys went on ignoring me and kept asking the girl her favorite color.

"You're jerks," I told them. "You don't get power by being obnoxious."

The girl was getting nervous, keeping one eye on them, one on me. I could tell that she was thinking, *which is worse, siding with the asshole boys making sexual jokes or siding with the weird girl I've never seen before in the blue lipstick?*

Well, that was an easy choice.

She whirled around and said, "Pink."

The boys laughed and high-fived. "Told you."

"Yeah."

"Ha ha."

You have to control your own world, I wanted so badly to tell the girl. *Don't hand them control. How they see you is up to you. Fight for it.*

We all went our separate ways.

Probably it didn't do any good to yell at them, but it made me feel better. Maybe they'll think twice before they do that again. But I doubt it.

Boys can be such losers, but that girl was weak, too.

I hope she knows how to box.

Chapter 22

by Diana: The Suspension—Part I

When you're an outsider in middle school, it feels as if everyone is against you.

If you're a kid like Hana, though, at least the grown-ups don't pile on. For example, Hana's art teachers slipped her scholarships every semester to an art college downtown for Saturday classes. She was the darling of her excellent costume crew teacher, who trusted her with interesting, challenging, and very fun projects, like the time Hana made forty Oompah-loompah hats for *Charlie and the Chocolate Factory*, fake hair included. She was getting straight A's and was beloved by her teachers. She even made her English teacher (a man!) cry with an impassioned book report project.

"This is why I teach," Hana heard him say to another teacher as he excused himself into the hall to wipe his eyes.

Yes, at least the grownups were on her side. Which is why Hana had a tremendous amount of respect and felt a sense of gratitude and kindness toward them.

At least, that was true until the day she was suspended from school on a trumped up weapons charge.

I was at home, working on a particularly thorny plot issue on my latest manuscript when the call came in. I had all my writing books out, including my absolute favorite, *Save the Cat*, by the late Blake Robbins.

The title comes from one of Blake's rules of screenwriting. The idea is that early on in a movie or a book, the hero has to be faced with a moral dilemma. His choice is to follow a rule, or to follow his heart and do what he knows is morally right, damn the rule. The hero must always do the morally correct thing and thereby save an innocent. He or she must never pass up an opportunity to save the cat. If he kills the cat, the audience is lost because it knows there will be no moral compass to this story. No center.

My phone rang. "Mrs. Holquist? This is Mary Chase, Vice Principal at the Middle School."

"Oh. Hi." My mind was racing. I instantly thought of Isaiah, who could definitely have gotten into a fistfight with the right provocation.

Wait—he wasn't in middle school. Wrong vice principal.

"I have Hana here with me."

"Hana?" I asked, surely sounding as if I had never heard of such a child. Hana was a tiger, but a silent, stealthy one lurking in the undergrowth, hardly noticed. She was never a rule-breaker.

"Yes." Long pause. "Mrs. Holquist, this is very serious."

My heart was pumping out of my chest. My hands had gone clammy. I had absolutely no capacity to imagine what Hana could have possibly done wrong, Mother Theresa in the clink.

"I was at lunch today," Mary said. "And I saw Hana with a knife."

"A knife?"

"Yes. It was a butter knife."

"A butter knife?" I wasn't following.

"She said she was using it to spread her peanut butter. On her crackers."

Oh my God. This was a peanut allergy issue. Did someone die? I was beside myself with dread as I tried to remember the peanut rules. Oh, poor Hana, having to deal with this. She'd never be the same, knowing that her snack was responsible for the death of a peer. Tears welled in my eyes.

"Knives are weapons," Dr. Chase continued.

"Excuse me?"

"Knives. This is about her knife, Mrs. Holquist."

I almost laughed out loud with relief. "Her butter knife? In her lunch? For her peanut butter?"

"All knives are forbidden. It's in the handbook."

"You're kidding me, right?" I asked, giddy with relief.

This was obviously not the proper response to this "serious" situation. After a bit more discussion, I realized that death by peanut allergy would have been an excusable accident. But packing—and I do mean packing—a butter knife in your lunch box to spread peanut butter was considered the direct equivalent to carrying a shotgun.

Zero tolerance.

I was at the school in a minute flat. *Don't say anything, don't say anything,* I told myself over and over. If I got started with this woman, I knew I wouldn't be able to stop.

Hana was sitting in Mary Chase's office, looking a little dazed in her fitted jacket and skinny jeans. Ms. Chase asked me if I wanted to sit.

"I have absolutely nothing to say to you," I told her in my flattest, I'm-going-home-to-call-my-attorney voice. "I'm taking Hana home now."

But she wasn't going to let us off that easy.

She started in on how there was a clear no-knife policy in the student handbook. Had we read the student handbook? "We can't allow students—any student—to break these important rules that exist for everyone's safety, including Hana's."

I was losing my cool, but Hana was positively serene, not angry or upset at all. In fact, she looked a little annoyed at me.

Mary explained that she'd looked at Hana's school record—straight A's.

"Yes. I know."

She said she'd talked to Hana, and Hana had told her that she'd packed her own lunch today, just as she had every morning for the last two years. "That's wonderful that she's so independent!"

She's not anymore, I thought.

Mary was happy to report that she saw on the transcript that Hana didn't have any other disciplinary problems.

Not yet. But if the grownups in charge like you keep up this nonsense, just you wait, lady.

She saw that Hana was involved in costume crew, a fine endeavor! Wonderful!

I stared at her, waiting for her to let us leave. *Don't say anything, don't say anything. There's nothing to say to a woman like this.* The cat was dead. Mary Chase had slaughtered it and proudly hung its hide up to dry. If the adults turned against Hana she might lose hope. If there was ever a time to save an innocent, this was it.

This cat, however, was sitting peacefully, oblivious, as cats often are.

"So I spoke to Mr. Barnes, our principal. In light of Hana's ignorance of the school's policy, her good record, and the fact that she obviously didn't mean any harm, we're going to suspend her for only one day. She'll still be allowed to participate in after-school activities, which are usually banned for the next two weeks."

"If you want me to thank you for that, it's not going to happen," I said as calmly as I could. "Can we go now?"

"If you have no further questions."

How do you sleep at night? Is this really what they pay you for? Do you know anything about children? Anything at all?

Hana and I left. In the empty hallway outside the office I said from between gritted teeth, "Let's get out of here. C'mon. We'll get ice cream. We'll eat it with knives."

"But I have French," Hana said. "I don't want to miss French."

"You hate French."

"I know. But I still don't want to miss it. Plus, then I have costume crew. I can't miss that."

"The suspension doesn't start until tomorrow," I said, thinking of the costume crew room, a veritable armory. "You really want to stay? You don't have to. Come on, we'll go get a slice of molten chocolate cake at Carbonne's. That woman is a moron."

"You were mean to her."

"She deserved it."

"It's still not right to be mean."

So I left alone, confused. Why was Hana standing up for that woman? Did she not understand the severity of what had just occurred?

When Hana got home just before dinner, she was still mad at me. "You shouldn't have been so mean to her," Hana said, picking up where we'd left off.

"Why not?"

"Did you see all that diet soda and all those awful diet muffin things in her office? There were cases of those things."

It took a while for me to grasp Hana's point: a woman who ate processed junk might not understand home-prepared food and the necessity of knives in lunches to keep real peanut butter from getting real crackers soggy.

"She told me to use the plastic knives in the cafeteria from now on," Hana continued with dismay.

"So. Ok. Do it."

"I can't use plastic that I have to throw away just because the school is scared of a butter knife. It's so wasteful. I guess I could take them home and wash them every day."

But there was more.

"Remember that kid who thought that Catkin was trying to eat him when he was really trying to bite him?" she asked. "He reminds me of Ms. Chase."

I thought back to the day when that odd boy had followed my son home. Isaiah and his friends had dashed upstairs, but the boy had stopped in the kitchen to pet the cat.

This was a cat who didn't need saving. He would have none of this petting-by-a-stranger nonsense. Annoyed, he tried to bite the boy's hand.

But the boy just laughed and cried out, "Your cat is trying to eat me! He thinks he can!"

"Please don't pet the cat. He's trying to show you he's angry," I explained. Hana watched, transfixed.

"He's trying to eat me!" The boy had laughed.

"Please stop!"

"He must think I'm food!"

It didn't end well.

Later, I explained to an incredulous Hana that some people have the kind of brain that makes it so that they can't understand intentions. "They take everything literally. For example, the cat biting his hand must mean the cat wants to eat him. You could tell he was a little off, right?"

"I think Ms. Chase is one of those people who take everything literally," Hana explained about the vice principal. "She thought my knife was a weapon because it had the same name as a weapon."

"So you're saying you feel bad for her?"

"Don't you?"

Actually, after talking to Hana, I sort of did.

That was when I realized that I had it all wrong. Hana wasn't the innocent who needed saving. Hana was the one with the moral compass. She was the hero of the story. Because while I had wanted to throttle the lady, Hana had recognized her as a naive innocent, unable to know how best to live in this world, and she took pity.

She'd been trying to save the cat.

Chapter 23

by Hana: The Suspension—Part II

I know I'm giving my mother a really hard time in this book. So this chapter, I'm going to give her a shout-out. (Don't get used to it, Mom.)

She was so mad about the suspension. She was much madder than I was. I was mostly confused. It was so dumb.

Anyway, when she gets mad, she writes.

So she wrote this letter, just for me.

We never sent it (we're not stupid).

But it still hangs on my wall.

Sometimes, you have to respect and honor your teachers and the people in charge. Other times, you really, really don't.

Without further ado, the letter:

> To: Whom It May Concern
> From: The Parents of Hana Holquist
> Re: Suspension of Hana Holquist for possession of weapon at school
>
> Oct. 29, 2009
>
> We have received your letter of Oct. 21, 2009 explaining our daughter Hana's one-day suspension for possession of a weapon. Since your letter indicates that a suspension is recorded on a student's disciplinary record forever, we wish to provide a fuller account of the reason for her suspension

and ask that this letter be included in her record.

First, respectfully, the facts. Hana put a dull, small butter knife in her lunchbox to spread peanut butter on her crackers. Surely, there's a difference between a weapon and a utensil even when they have the same name.

Hana is coming to lunch next week with an egg beater. Yeah, I said beater. What're you gonna do about that one, smart guys? Don't see that in the Handbook.

The week after that, a colander. (You do the anagram!)

Second, we wish to emphasize that under no circumstances did Hana intend this eating utensil as a weapon. However, to support your crusade against everyday objects that might be dangerous, she has decided to join the fearless administrators at _____ Middle School in their crusade for fail safe schools. We hope you like her campaign to re-name the fork *the stabber*, the spoon *the gouger*, and the ball-point pen *the crotch-spear*. We are certain you'll support her in her endeavor for increased safety and hope you enjoy the posters she is hanging in the main lobby. I thought they were a tad morbid, but in the face of what could happen (it hasn't happened yet, but it could), I had to agree with everything but the glitter in the pools of blood.

As a former advertising copywriter, I can attest to the efficacy of the headline, *Cutlery Kills!*

Unfortunately, Vice Principal Chase's explanation that Hana's punishment was to miss a day of school confused Hana yet again. She concluded that Vice Principal Chase understood children even less than she understood cutlery. She'd like to thank everyone at _____ Middle School for her day off. She went out for sushi (you should've seen those guys' knives, baby), then a matinee showing of *Cloudy with a Chance of Meatballs*. The irony of seeing a movie about a crazed inventor who destroyed a town with extremely dangerous meatballs was not lost on Hana.

As to Vice Principal Chase's suggestion that in the future Hana use the plastic utensils supplied by the cafeteria, Hana would like to point out that there is a pile of plastic waste at the bottom of the ocean bigger than Europe, and she will not in her good conscious contribute to it. Please try not to worry about her eating with her fingers.

Unarmed, as it were.

If she needs to defend herself against some sixth grade nut-job with a stabber, she'll use her crotch-spear. (N.b.: For defensive purposes only, this is in no way a threat.)

We would also like to thank Vice Principal Chase for limiting Hana's three-day suspension to just one day. We do, however, still consider Vice Principal Chase a morally weak and therefore untrustworthy adult who has no compunction about setting this insane process in motion even though she know the unjust, out-of-control consequence. Therefore due to Vice Principal Chase's incredible lack of common or moral sense, we will consider her a moron for the full duration of our daughter's middle school career, perhaps even beyond. That's 376 days, but who's counting?

We'd also like to offer unending thanks for allowing our daughter to continue to participate in costume crew for the fall play. She left Vice Principal Chase's office properly chastised for her butter knife, then proceeded to the costume room where she cut with sharp scissors, sewed with pins and needles, and even ironed.

With steam.

She didn't—for obvious reasons—go near the glue guns.

May everyone in the administration at _____ Middle School survive the jungle that is life among the tweens another year. We all feel safe with the likes of you guarding our children from hooligans, scoundrels, and healthy, responsible eaters.

God bless America.

Sincerely,

Peter and Diana Holquist

(P.S.—Watch out for costume crew—they are armed and dangerous!)

Chapter 24

by Diana: Soccer—Part I

What's a tale of middle school woes without a nice dose of sibling rivalry?

As Hana continued to be abused by the world around her, Isaiah cruised. Sometimes it seemed as if he existed under a ray of permanent sunshine. He was consistently excellent at school with very little effort. He had an abundance of friends. And he was getting scary good at soccer.

It got to the point that he was playing soccer just about every day. At any given time, he might be on three or four teams: his Academy team, his futsal team (indoor Brazilian-style soccer played with a small, heavy ball), his 3v3 team (fast-paced three-on-three soccer on a small field), and the Union Juniors (the developmental team for the Philadelphia Union Major League Soccer team).

Oh, had I mentioned the Union Juniors before? Sorry. Won't bring it up again.

Like most not-fully-reformed tiger mothers, I still struggled with a tiny little status problem.

I didn't know anything about soccer. I tried, I really did. But the game was simultaneously too boring and too fast for me. I couldn't follow it, no matter how hard I concentrated. For example, during Isaiah's U-10 season (that means the boys are under ten: nine-year-olds), I dedicated myself to understanding and recognizing offsides. In soccer, the offsides line moves with the defenders and is timed by the release of the ball from a teammate's boot.

Why they called their shoes "boots" was another thing I didn't in any way understand, but it made me feel cool to use the lingo.

Anyway, I watched instructional videos on YouTube. I watched professional games. I watched the boys play.

After the whole season, I still couldn't call offsides even when it was obvious to the pre-schoolers watching with me on the sidelines.

As Isaiah (and therefore I) got deeper and deeper into the soccer world, I knew I had to do something in order to learn this game. The other parents indulged in constant analysis of the players, while I often said things like, "They're all just so darn cute out there," earning me universal scorn.

Playing soccer was out of the question. I was too fat and slow. So I made a new plan. I'd watch Isaiah's games, then write them up from my point of view. Afterward, I'd interview other people who'd watched or played the game, and I'd try to synthesize what they'd seen and I'd missed. After a season of this, surely, I'd start to understand the subtleties. Or at the very least, the rules.

So, after the first game of the U-11 season, I typed up my notes. Then I interviewed Isaiah to get his take. After I'd typed up that, Hana said, "I was there. Why don't you interview me, too?"

"You didn't even watch," Isaiah pointed out. "You were reading and walking around. You don't even know who won."

"Who won?" she asked. But before he could answer she held up a hand. "Wait—don't tell me. I don't care."

"See?" he insisted.

"You should still interview me," she said. "I spent a day there, after all."

She had a point.

Here's what you need to know about Hana and soccer: she knows even less than me.

Here's what you need to know about soccer and me: my rapidly-growing ability to keep my emotions and anxiety out of Hana's life was in part made possible by my being able to let them all out elsewhere. Specifically, on the sidelines of Isaiah's soccer games.

Sometimes the best thing that can happen to a child is that the parent's insanity gets focused on a sibling.

This is my interpretation of one game. I think it gives excellent insight into my delicate, deteriorating state of mind at this difficult time in our lives.

Game 1, Division 1 Elite,
_____ Soccer Club vs. _____

I have made a pact with myself. I will not scream like a crazy person. I will not say anything unkind about any child, especially those children whose parents are within earshot. I will watch the game calmly, detached, as if I were a rational observer. I will watch both sides equally. I will not focus on my child, except when he's involved in play. I will not swear at my child, even under my breath.

I will not damn him to hell.

But as I unfold my forest-green chair with the handy built-in cup holders (as if I could drink at a moment like this—maybe vodka) I notice that the other team is unnaturally tall. I despise them for this, as if their exceptional size was a sign of small moral worth. *Don't hate young children.* I know, I know. It's wrong. And yet, the hatred of the other team is already a taste, a smell, a thing awakening inside me like an animal.

An animal with sharp, grippy claws and beady little eyes.

We're not tiger mothers, we're reptilian. Or worse, rodents.

The teams warm up. The mutant giants on the other team kick the ball to each other with considerable skill. This feels unjust. We're supposed to be the best. After all, we're a step above an A-team. *We're regional.* We're the boys skimmed off the top of the local A-teams. *We're Academy.*

By "we," naturally, I don't mean me. I mean the boys. I could very well pull a muscle reaching down to get my Dunkin' Donuts glazed cruller out of my cooler.

I look down the field to Isaiah's team. They shrink before my eyes into helpless, tiny little things, fluttering around a soccer ball that seems to come up to their knees.

To control my anxiety, I try to take notes so I can keep track of the game. But what month is it? What day? What year? I can't focus. My grip on the pencil is turning my fingers white. Who is this team again? Whoever they are, they don't deserve to win. They deserve to lose and lose hard. Someone has to put those overgrown monsters in their place and what pleasure that it will be us.

I am so hyped, I have managed to get only the date (just one day off) onto my pad as the boys break their huddle and take the field. My throat is dry with anticipation.

I am determined to remain calm. In order to do this, I will concentrate on two things. First, how the other team plays what Isaiah calls with supreme derision, "boot and chase." That is, they let loose huge kicks and then hope to be able to chase them down. "No skill," Isaiah says. "Ugly soccer." Also, I'm to watch how Isaiah's team is struggling in the midfield. (He's a defender.)

"Notice how we can't hold position in the midfield," he told me. "It's killing us."

This is confusing to me because the midfield is both a place (the middle of the field) and a position (the three or four boys who play in front of the defense, but behind the strikers). I have to remember later to ask Isaiah which he means, the people or the place, but now it's too late. The whistle blows and the game begins.

Two kicks into the game, I'm lost. I try to whisper under my breath so I can keep track of the flow of play. "Right back to right mid to—oooh. That can't be good." Muttering *not good* near the parents of the boy who has lost the ball is, well, not good.

The dad pacing behind me coughs and scowls.

The other team scores.

I have no idea how the goal happened. If pressed, I might say, "We were looking good, then bam! Bad!" When talking soccer, I have the vocabulary and understanding of a three-year-old. I am beginning to see that fixing this is going to be a long, hard road.

"Who scored?" I ask the mother to my right.

"I think it was the big one in the midfield," she says.

"The position or the player?"

"What?"

"Huh?"

None of us have a clue.

At half-time, we're still down 1-0.

I'm distraught. Pure emotion. Wrung out. It wasn't supposed to be this way. Why not? Here's my nuanced analysis: We can't lose because we're special.

Apparently, not as special as the other team.

Game on.

More running. More shouting. I've given up taking notes. In fact, I have no idea where my pad and pencil are. It's entirely possible I've eaten them. "You're better than these guys!" I shout at our team, even though "these guys" are standing right in front of me, and they're sweet-faced ten-year-olds. I'm aware that I'm acting badly, but I want "these guys" to know that even if they win, they don't deserve to. We do. Something about "dump and chase" and boots that aren't boots and illegal growth hormones.

If we lose, it'll be unjust. There must be something wrong. It must be someone's fault. I begin looking around for culprits.

"What a terrible field," I hear one father say as his son goes down.

I hadn't noticed, but he's right! Who could score on a field like this?

"Stupid official. Why do we always get the blind ones?"

Then I hear whisperings from the group of dads I once heard a coach derisively call *The Brain Trust.* "Why is he playing V. up top?...V's hopeless at striker... Can't score to save his life...What is he thinking?...No, it's not V's fault, Isaiah let it in."

Isaiah? Oh, no! I'm pretty sure the ball did go in from the right and he's the right defender. Oh, Isaiah! (He'd explain to me later it was a three-on-one and neither the goalie nor he had a chance. I hadn't noticed. How can you count the offense? There's no time; they come so fast.)

I try to be rational, but the snarling momma rat—I mean tiger—at the center of my soul is not a rational being. The heart of my dilemma is simply this: reality is not conforming to my fantasy.

This makes me angry.

Anger feels good.

It feels.

I am middle aged. I work all the time at my computer, not seeing another living soul. I never get to scream, to yell, to shout, to be an animal—a Tiger as it were. Except when I'm around my children.

I know it's wrong to yell, to indulge in these narcissistic rages. But no matter. Because when the kids are so little, there's something much more important than the present: the future.

It's okay if the present reality doesn't exactly line up with my hopes and dreams. Anything is possible in the future. It's okay if I behave like a maniac in the present, because, you see, I'm only thinking of the future.

My mind is racing. Isaiah needs a new coach. A new team. He needs new hundred dollar baby kangaroo-skin soccer boots. (Yes, Virginia, they make soccer cleats out of baby kangaroos. I have no idea why.)

The final whistle.

1-1 tie.

I gather my emotions, drifting back to reality like a popped balloon back to earth. I tell my son, "I thought you guys looked good out there."

He grimaces. He knows that his dear, excitable mother didn't have a clue.

Chapter 25

by Hana: Soccer—Part II

If you ever want to know how absurd a soccer mother is, search "crazy soccer mom" on YouTube. There are always excellent videos to demonstrate. I make my mother watch them sometimes, just to calm her down.

Anyway, when it comes to soccer, I show up for the stuff I can get out of it. Hot chocolate. Maybe a garage sale that we pass on the drive in. A good forest behind the fields to explore. Once, there was even a Wegmans grocery store with its excellent food court. I love Wegmans. That was a great tournament.

This game, I get the hot chocolate and a multi-family garage sale while the teams warm up. I pick up a book I'd wanted to read for a while, Mitch Album's *The Five People You Meet in Heaven,* so I'm happy. I sit by my mom a bit, but now the game's started and she's cursing out my brother under her breath, and I'm embarrassed that she's swearing.

"Stop swearing, Mom."

"Sorry, I'm so nervous."

"It's a game of ten-year-olds. Get a life."

I move away to the shade. But then I get too cold and I'm tired of reading, so I move back into the sun and close my eyes and listen to the parents yell.

Go. GO. GOOOOOOOO!

Oh. OH. OOOOOOOOH!

It's kind of got a nice rhythm.

The boys are still chasing that stupid ball. Here's everything you need to know about soccer: it never ends. No really, I mean it. Never. Year-round, every-day, a nightmare you can't wake up from.

I take a walk in the woods and see a baby fox. First, I think it's cute. Then, I think that maybe Mom and Dad fox are nearby and I've wandered into their nesting area and they're going to attack me. No one will hear my death cries over the mad screaming of the soccer parents.

I go back to the sidelines. Wouldn't it be great if the foxes came out here, ran around a bit, freaked everyone out? There was a hunter's blind set up in the woods, and I imagine being a hunter, trying to shoot out the soccer balls. Now that would be a sport I wouldn't mind trying.

I crochet a few octopuses, just for fun. They come out pretty good. I love how the tentacles naturally twirl.

The two teams slap hands. I have no idea who won, and I don't care. No, that's not entirely true. I hope they lost. Make my stupid brother mad.

The boys come over to the parents, and the parents lie about how awesome they played, even though they've been muttering and cursing about them for the past hour and it turns out that they only tied some loser team from the middle of nowhere.

On the drive home, my mom and my brother have the exact same conversation that they always have. *This one should have done this. That one should have done that.* As if my mother has a clue. The whole time, she's on the sidelines going, "Wait. What? What just happened? GOOOOOOO BLUUUUUUUE!!!!!"

But she's busy talking to Isaiah, so I can space out the window and enjoy myself.

It wasn't a bad day, all in all. Watching soccer is kind of like a day at the beach. Relaxing and productive. Plus, what's cooler than seeing a baby fox and reading a great book and getting a little handwork in? Soccer games are like life: you have to find what's good, and ignore the rest.

Chapter 26

by Diana: The Sleep Over

Hana pleaded with me to be a chaperone at the end-of-year, seventh grade sleepover trip to a campground a couple of hours away.

I thought of the overnight birthday party back in sixth grade, and I begged her not to ask this impossible task of me. This year for her birthday, we'd taken one friend to see *Wicked*, the musical about the green outcast who is much smarter and funnier than the popular girls, but shunned because of her green skin. I highly recommend it.

"They can't get enough moms. They'll need to cancel the trip," she told me. "You can come!" she said. "You don't have a job."

"I do. I just do it at home."

"Whatever. Come." She didn't really believe I had a job.

Memories of Hana's twelfth birthday party still made me twitch. This camping trip was a two-hour bus ride, four meal, overnight extravaganza. "I don't think I can do it."

But of course, I gave in and I went. I was too curious to watch Hana in her natural habitat not to. I was interested in her world. I wanted to understand it.

By the time we got to the campsite, I was toast. My head ached from the bouncy bus and its unbelievably loud passengers.

"See what I have to live with every day?" Hana asked.

I met the bunk—twelve girls whom I was responsible for until tomorrow. They were very polite. I recognized a few of them, but not many. They unpacked, picked their bunks. Hana, as usual, was off in a corner, as alone as you can get in a room packed with tweens.

The day was filled with "team building" activities in small groups. For the first one, they had to get the whole group across three wooden platforms with a few flimsy props without touching the ground. The alpha boy of the group was bossing everyone around. A scrawny boy with glasses kept mumbling just quietly enough so he couldn't be heard by anyone but me, "That's not physically possible. It won't work."

"Do the girls ever speak?" I asked the counselor.

"It's always like this," she said. "They let the boys lead, even though they fail and fail and fail."

"That is so depressing."

"I know," she sighed as we watched the boys tumble off the bridge for the umpteenth time. "It's like Wall Street."

Finally, the nerdy boys took over and got the job done.

Then there were meals, free time, until finally we trundled back to the bunks for lights out.

"We're going to stay up all night!" the prettiest girl yelled. Then she looked right at me.

"I'm going to bed," I said, even though I knew this would be impossible. I had been begging ibuprofen from every parent I crossed paths with like a crazed addict, but it hadn't made a dent. "You guys can do what you like, so long as you don't leave the bunk or break the rules." *Please survive the night. Only recreational drugs. Only consensual sex with disease-free boys.*

The girls spent an unbelievable amount of time getting ready for bed.

A tiny, impossibly thin girl had brought bug spray, and she was spraying it on every surface.

"Hey, take it easy with that stuff," I said. "It's poison. We're inside."

"I hate bugs. I can't sleep near bugs." She kept spraying and spraying. I tried not to breathe.

One nervous girl in the corner was folding and refolding all her clothes. She had brought an enormous bag with her and I counted four pairs of jeans for the overnight trip aside from the pair she was wearing. I realized she hadn't brought anything to sleep in.

"Shorts make fine pajamas," I told her.

She turned bright red and looked away.

They were all desperate to call their mothers, but despite their iPhones, no one could get reception.

When they were finally scrubbed and changed, they formed a circle in the middle of the floor and played whisper-down-the-lane, the child's game where one girl whispers something into the ear of the girl next to her, and so on and so on until the last person in the circle says the now-modified, misheard phrase out loud to great hilarity.

"Dr. Seuss loves cupcakes with bran?"

"No! It was Suzie loves Kevin Overman!"

I was beside myself with shock at the little-kid's game. Whisper-down-the-lane? Really? Were these girls as terrified of their night as I was?

Hana didn't join the game. She said she was exhausted, and climbed into her bunk.

Naturally, I was furious at her for this. Why wouldn't she try to fit in? Didn't she see that this was a social opportunity?

She was out within two minutes. Proof yet again that social pressure meant nothing to her.

The remaining eleven girls were yawning and gamely trying to stay up. Some of them looked like they were in physical pain.

They switched to truth or dare. This game, apparently, was now played with an app. They got out their iPhones, but no one could get reception, no matter how far they hung out the windows or crouched in the corners. They were undone. How did you play truth or dare without electronics?

They tried other activities, but one by one the girls bowed out of the games and climbed into their bunks until there were only three girls left.

The three climbed into one bunk to talk about boys.

They thought I was asleep. I wished I were asleep.

One said that her boyfriend scared her.

"He never smiles," another pointed out, agreeing.

"Yeah," the third chimed in. "It's kind of creepy."

The first girl gathered a stuffed animal into her arms. It started to play a song.

"Is your teddy bear singing?" one asked. *One Day My Prince Will Come* drifted over the cabin.

"So?"

"That's stupid."

"I like it."

"Are you going to keep going out with him?"

"I guess. I wish he wasn't so scary. He makes me so uncomfortable."

"Me, too."

"But he's so cute."

"I know. I just wish he'd smile sometimes, you know?"

The bear ended its song into the silence that had descended on them.

And they quietly drifted off to sleep after all.

PART III: A Tiger Is Born

"Rabbi Zusya...said, a short while before his death:
'In the world to come I shall not be asked: *Why were you not Moses?*
I shall be asked: *Why were you not Zusya?*'"

--Martin Buber, *The Way of Man*

Chapter 27

by Diana: 8th Grade Begins

After seventh grade, Hana spent her summer as a counselor-in-training at a handcrafts camp for sewing, knitting, crocheting, and needle felting. The place attracted teachers and kids who thought that a summer sitting inside all day, not talking much, and concentrating on intricate handwork was fun.

In other words, it was Hana's kind of place.

She arrived at 8:30 in the morning and stayed till four. She was entranced by the teachers. She wanted to be like Miss Nora, the joyous woman who lived with her mother and sewed all her own clothes. Or Miss Toni, the friendly manager who always knew how to fix a seam or cast off a difficult knitting project.

Now Hana was Miss Hana in her apron, sweeping the floor or ironing a child's wobbly-cut project. She hated to leave. The little kids were amazed at her pink hair extensions and rainbow braces. The teachers loved that she was so soft-spoken and helpful.

"How's she doing?" I asked.

"You know Hana," one of the lead teachers told me. "She always needs to be the center of attention."

We laughed, because of course, Hana was the complete opposite. She was competent, responsible, and hardworking—an amazing combination of traits in a thirteen-year-old girl. The last thing she wanted was attention.

"I hope she's not too quiet," I said.

"She has a powerful presence," Miss Toni said.

I couldn't think of a higher compliment. The very opposite of the conventional tween.

Her friends came home from their nine thousand dollar summer camps, breathless and giddy and bronzed.

Hana was composed, pale as a specter, and thoughtful. She was spinning off in the opposite direction of her peers. She looked like another species when I'd see her in the midst of a group of pre-teens.

Okay, never in the group. She floated outside the circle, watching, thinking.

I probably don't have to tell you that this caused me considerable anxiety. I'd watch the girls with their arms thrown around one another, their faces lit with the joy of belonging, and I'd wonder if Hana craved that kind of closeness the way I craved it for her.

But even when she'd have girls over, or be invited somewhere, which happened more and more often, still she hung back. Just as she had three years ago at Halloween, she still disliked the group more than she disliked being alone. This was her perfectly valid, consistent position. This was her. Ironically, I felt the exact same way about my life. And yet, this trait in Hana drove me to distraction.

As eighth grade began, my anxiety focused on the outward symbol of her solitary lifestyle: her lack of a cell phone. Don't get me wrong, she had a cell phone. How cruel a mother do you think I am? She just refused to use it. Her friends, meanwhile, were texting, instant messaging, Skyping, and Facebooking. By the end of September, it became too uncool to call a landline, and her friends refused to call the house. "I don't want to have to talk to your mother," they'd say. "Turn on your cell."

But her hatred of technology trumped everything. She wouldn't use her phone. She didn't care. "If they really have a reason to call, they'll call the house."

But of course they didn't.

One of her friends came over one afternoon and signed her up for a Facebook account.

I was insanely relieved.

Now at least she had some way to communicate that was "cool." Not that she communicated much. I thought it was a spelling issue, as her spelling was still abysmal. But on-line-speak didn't have to be spelled correctly. In fact, the more badly spelled, the cooler it was.

Other mothers thought I was some kind of cruel tyrant when they found out that she didn't text. "She's going to be left behind," they'd tell me, an urgency I recognized all too well on their faces. "You must make her use her phone!"

What could I do? Force her to text? "Type LOL! Just type it! LOL, damn it! Now hit send! Come on, for God's sake! I'm going to ground you for the whole month!" Was there a tutor I could hire for this? The situation was absurd. "You're going to be left behind," I told her.

"Where do you hear these stupid things?" Hana asked.

A mother of one of Isaiah's friends admitted to me that she sometimes snuck her son's phone and sent fake texts to his friends, pretending to be the boy, just to get the conversation started.

I couldn't go that far, but I could get just involved enough to make myself crazy. Hana might not have done much on Facebook, but I became a stalker. Facebook was a terrifying glimpse into the world of these children. They'd post everything, from screenshots of their failing grades to pictures of themselves in bikinis on the beach, their butts stuck out like centerfold models.

With Facebook, I was done wondering what Hana was being left out of; I could see it. A social event would happen, then happen all over again online.

"I had so much fun last night with Sophie, Lauren, Jodi and Sue!" Lani would post, usually with pictures of smiling, laughing girls as proof. Obscure references to inside jokes would follow in the comment stream. "Wafffflez!!!!" "Ahahahahahah!!" "Looozerz cuteeee!!!!"

Where had Hana been that night? What did she think when she saw these posts?

She'd been in her room, sewing. Apparently, she didn't think much.

"You can tell the desperate kids, because they post everything," she'd say. "It's like it's their diary and they need everyone to read it."

It was an astute analysis.

But was home a safe place when these windows into the bigger world were open, letting in the laughter and music?

When another child posted that she was suspended because she cheated on a test, I was shocked. "Who is this girl? Doesn't she know not to post these things? Then a boy named Brian commented that he cheated on the test, too. Then Lucy said that everyone cheated on it.

"Why would they post that for the world to see?" I asked Hana

"Why not? No one cares."

"I care."

"The mothers who have nothing better to do than stalk their kids' Facebooks care," she pointed out.

I didn't have to worry about Hana posting anything private, because she didn't post much of anything. She was busy all the time sewing or working on one project or another. She was becoming alarmingly independent.

It drove me mad.

As she drifted further and further out of the mainstream, it became harder and harder to talk about her achievements. There was nothing measurable or socially acceptable I could point to as proof of her worth.

She is herself fully and truly.

How lame did that sound?

She is like no one else.

Indeed.

The life she was building was complex, solitary, and unique.

There wasn't a prize for that. Rather, that sort of behavior was punished at every turn. There was no way to cheer for that from the sidelines, to rant and rave about it. Stories about the triumphs of solitude and quiet contemplation fell flat.

When other mothers crowed about awards and honors their children won, I kept my mouth shut.

My kid is really, really good at thrifting. It's hard to explain. You have to see it to understand.

My kid can throw a mean left hook.

My kid can sit in her room for hours, absorbed, without electronics.

My kid doesn't care what your kid thinks of her.

It was strangely intriguing, a child like this.

One afternoon, we dropped Isaiah off at the Union training fields. I hated watching Union training, as the competition on the field was ferocious to the point of brutal. Also, the other parents were always trolling for information about the soccer world that they could use for barter or revenge. The situation gave me hives. It was impossible not to get caught up in the fever of it.

Hana and I drove to the mall across the highway. But as we walked through the parking lot, I began to feel the exact same tightening in my gut that I had felt on the soccer field a moment before. It was as if we were walking onto another field of battle, preparing for a whole different kind of competition.

But what was she competing at?

Her uniform today was a high-waisted red polka dot skirt, grey T-shirt, white tights, black flats, and light blue lipstick. Her braces were teal. Her long, wavy blonde hair was pulled into a messy bun. She was five foot two. She might have weighed ninety pounds.

We walked through the mall to H&M, her head held high, me a step behind, watching in wonder. Groups of kids passed her and sniggered and chortled. Heads turned. Something inside me curled up: *she can't win at this game.*

At H&M, I drifted around the store, bored, watching the girls in their little groups. Here in their natural habitat, it was impossible not to notice their awkward sameness. They circled the clothes, hesitatingly. *What do you think of this? Do I look fat in this? How do you wear this?* They all wore the same thing, had the same hair style, the same makeup. They watched each other carefully. If I spied on a group long enough (thirty seconds), I'd figure out the pecking order. There was always a pecking order.

All at once, I saw the world through Hana's eyes. *Yes, you do look fat in that and you look like everyone else and for God's sake, don't buy that because you already own it ten times over can't you find something original and why do you follow that girl? She's not being nice to you.*

Hana was in a corner, talking to a clerk, a flamboyant boy in skinny jeans and a silver sparkling shirt. I snuck up on the other side of the rack just in time to overhear him say, "Everyone is talking about how much they love your skirt."

"Thanks." She smiled demurely.

She scores! One to nothing, advantage Hana.

"Where did you get that lipstick?" another girl asks her a few minutes later. I'm spying from behind the sale rack.

"It's Lime Crime."

"I thought so. I *looove* Lime Crime."

"I know." They talked about lipstick for a while.

"I don't think I could wear it, though," the girl said as Hana started to move away. H&M was serious business, and Hana knew we had a time limit to get back to pick up her brother.

"Oh, I think you could. You'd look good," Hana said. "You should at least try it."

"I couldn't." The other girl shook her head, but she smiled, happier than she'd been a moment before.

Two to nothing.

Hana stood in the dressing room line with her two carefully selected items behind girls with their arms heaped with unexamined, uninspired choices. They eyed her selections. Eyed her. Looked away. Looked back.

She really did look strikingly amazing in the midst of all the sameness.

"That's a great sweater. Where did you find it?" one girl asked her, nodding at one of the two pieces Hana had found worthy of trying on.

"I think it was the last one," Hana said. "From the sale rack."

The other girl looked a little mad. But what could she do?

By the time we left the store with Hana's one, absolutely perfect, unique, five-dollar sweater, I knew that Hana had won a decisive victory. Not the sweater. It wasn't about finding the perfect sweater any more than great soccer was about putting the ball in the net. It was about creativity, about zigging when the other guys zagged. It was about knowing exactly what you were going to do before you did it, then doing it flawlessly, leaving the other guy staring after you, confused. It was about loving what you did for the pure joy of the sport.

We piled back into the car and picked up Isaiah, bloody and so tired he can barely speak. He collapses in the back seat, sucking down what's left of his water. He looks like hell, but I can tell he did well from the tiny smile that plays over his lips as he stares out the window, reliving the battles of the previous two hours.

Hana is next to me, the same contented smile on her face.

And you know what? I'm smiling, too.

Chapter 28

by Hana: The Two Tutu Day

I bought two tutus from eBay. They were listed by my favorite blogger of all time, Doe Deere. She's a model and businesswoman with blue hair. She has her own makeup company. She created the company because no one made makeup in the colors she wanted. Anyway, Doe Deere decided to move from New York to California, and so she was selling some of her old stuff on line.

It's hard to find tutus in sizes bigger than toddler sizes that aren't for real ballerinas. The real ballerina tutus are really expensive. I won Doe Deere's pink tutu and her baby blue one, ten dollars and two cents for both, total. The two cents let me outbid the next highest bidder who stopped at ten dollars.

I was so happy.

I have to admit, I was a little nervous to wear the tutus to school. Even for me, they were a little out there. I hadn't expected them to be so short.

Did you know that tutu means "butt" in French? It's true. I swear. My French teacher told me. If you saw these tutus, you'd know why.

I posted on Facebook, asking people what they thought: should I wear them or shouldn't I? Everyone was for it. "Be yourself!" "Wear what you love!" "Yesssss!"

I was going for it.

I made a self-esteem sheet in case I lost my nerve. This is what it said:

> "You dress for you and only you. Take it to the next level. Sparkles. UNICORNS. Doing this takes a lot of courage. I am brave. Remember that this is really brave of you. Catkin. Cleo. Toby. [The names of my cats—they give me courage because they don't care what anyone thinks and I love them a lot.] Remember, *she* [Doe Deere] wore the tutu fairy skirts. If she can do it, I can! She would be proud of me. She had to wear her crazy things on the subway."

At breakfast that morning, my mother asked me, "Why two?"

"Because," I explained, "If you're going to go for it, you have to take it to the next level."

I was so puffy, I had trouble fitting through the stands at orchestra, so I had to crawl on my hands and knees to my seat.

Later that day, we had a severe weather drill. If a tornado or hurricane hits, we get into a hallway with no windows. We get down on our hands and knees and put our butts up in the air. I looked like a goose, with my three butts up in the air (mine, plus the two tutus).

"Now, all you girls who wear inappropriate things to school will maybe think twice," the teacher said. As if the girls who wore the short skirts cared that their butts were up in the air, hanging out for everyone to see.

"Bad day to wear my thong," Nick said.

Nick was hilarious. I would never get that awful image out of my head.

I was glad I had on my striped leggings. I was covered, at least.

In math, my friend Amy and I raised our hands at the same time. The teacher called on Amy.

"I need help with number two," she said.

The teacher said, "Hana, do you need help on two, too?" And then she laughed.

Two, too. Tutu.

I got it. It just wasn't funny.

I didn't like that teacher much.

My aunt was pregnant, and she said that everyone, even strangers, touched her stomach. She lived in New York City and rode the subway, so this could be disturbing.

That was what wearing the tutus was like. Everyone kept touching them, even strangers in the hallways.

Why? Why would you touch someone's clothes?

"You're wearing tutus," people said.

"Is that an observation or a judgment?" I asked. It was a line from a movie, but no one ever knew that.

"Um, er, an observation?"

"Good."

People kept asking me why I was wearing them.

I said, "Because I want to. Why are you wearing those jeans?"

No one knew what to say to that.

I could tell them the answer if I wanted to: you wear those jeans because you want to fit in. You look lousy in them. Your butt's too big, or too small, or you'd look really great in an A-line skirt, but you wouldn't dare, would you?

But I didn't tell them any of that. I didn't want to hurt their feelings. Anyway, they probably thought fitting in was a good thing to want.

But if you do it too long, you forget how to want anything but what everyone else wanted. It was just like little kids, wanting to make their mothers happy. Only in middle school, it was wanting to make your friends happy by following them.

Never follow.

Believe me, as weird as some people thought I was, a lot of kids liked what I did. I know because they told me.

I know when the popular girl comes up to me in the hall and asks where I got my lipstick, it was time for new lipstick, because I liked to have unique things.

I told her where I got it.

No problem. I was already moving on.

Chapter 29

by Diana: The Unicorn—Part I

Hana came downstairs for breakfast one morning wearing a unicorn hoodie and I knew it had gone too far.

The unicorn hoodie was bright pink. She'd bought the unadorned hoodie at Target, then made a rainbow colored mane out of six layers of fringed fleece that went down the back of the hood onto the back. On the top of the hood, proud and triumphant, was a horn also made out of fleece and stuffing. A long rainbow colored tail bounced behind her as she moved about the kitchen getting breakfast. The thing was gorgeous—spectacular, even.

But still, this was middle school.

Oh, sweet Mary mother of God.

When I resorted to Catholic prayers, you knew things were bad.

You are not wearing that to school, I wanted to proclaim.

Please, please, please, do not wear that to school, I wanted to beg.

But, as was my way, I bit my tongue. Hard.

When Hana went back upstairs, Isaiah's head dropped to the kitchen counter. "No. She can't. Oh, God."

He also knew better than to say anything within her hearing.

I waited out the day in tense apprehension, trying but failing to get some work done. When she came home, I commanded myself to stay in my office until she came upstairs.

I listened to my unicorn moving around the kitchen. Would her face be tear-streaked? Would she still be wearing the thing, or would she have kicked it into a storm sewer on her way home, humiliation and shame too ripe in her to be able to ever see it again?

Her footsteps clomped up the stairs. I tried to guess her emotional state from the sound.

"Hey," I said, still typing, not looking up. No over-emotional involvement here. "How was the day?"

"Okay." She plopped down in my comfy chair with a bowl of chocolate ice cream. The cat jumped on her lap, purring, hoping for a taste.

She was still wearing the hoodie, hood up despite the humid day.

"Don't get chocolate on it," I said. If I could somehow lurch across the room and spill her ice cream on the thing, could I claim it was stained beyond repair? Not likely, as she was the kind of kid who knew a thing or two about stain removal due to her love of Martha Stewart.

"So, tell me things," I said. My kids knew that I spent all day alone in my office and that they were therefore required to bring me news—any news at all—of the outside world as a kindness to their mother, the shut-in. No detail was too small. This was also my way of trying not to impose my own neurosis on their lives, as I badly wanted to grab them and demand, *Who did you eat lunch with what did you get on the science test what chair were you at orchestra this morning and for God's sake did you or did you not really walk to school with a child of the opposite sex like Joey's mother reported to me at the Acme and what did you say and what did he/she respond and should I be concerned because, honestly, he/she is not good enough for you!*

"Can we go to Target?" she asked.

"Why?" I kept my eyes on my computer screen.

"I need to buy four more hoodies."

"Four?"

"Kids ordered them. I have to get the fleece, too. Can we go to Joanne's Fabric this weekend?"

"Kids? Ordered—?" I cleared my throat. I spun my chair around to face her. "They want unicorn hoodies?"

"Kelly just wants hers to be a horse. I guess I'll make it brown. Maybe with white. She's really into horses." She looked up from her cat and ice cream. "Don't look so surprised. Everyone loved it. Why? What did you think would happen?"

"Me? Think? Nothing. I had no idea."

"So? Can we go?"

"No."

"Why not?"

"We have to find a cheaper hoodie supplier than Target."

She put down her bowl of ice cream. The cat jumped at it. "Why? Mine was like, maybe sixteen dollars. I'll sell the finished ones for way more."

"You have to buy the fleece, make sure you're compensated for your labor. You'd have to charge too much to make a profit."

She looked at me like I was nuts. "I'm making hoodies for my friends, not for profit."

"Right. But just think about it. If the hoodie is sixteen plus tax and the fabric is probably at least two dollars a yard plus tax and that's if it's on sale—"

She held up a hand to stop me. "Julie said she'd pay a hundred dollars."

"Oh." Well, that made things simpler. "Still, we have to think this through."

"Okay." She didn't care. She just wanted to get it going. That was fine. I could be her business manager. I could do the caring.

I could handle the math.

And the advertising...

I was starting to think big.

Chapter 30

by Hana: What I Wore—Part II

I started a blog to keep track of all the stuff I made and all the outfits I put together so I wouldn't forget. I decided to call it Hanacorn.

The name Hanacorn is a combination of my name, Hana, and a unicorn. I really like unicorns. In some ways they're sweet and beautiful. But at the same time, they're solitary animals who are majestic and regal.

The blog keeps track of stuff I make and stuff I buy. I'm not exactly sure what I want it to be, but for now it's just fun.

If you are wondering what a quadrapus is, it is a four legged octopus. This quadrapus has a mustache and a little bow tie. I made him for one of my friend's birthdays. I always make my friends stuffed animals for their birthdays as part of their presents.

This is a shirt that I made from an old Halloween costume that I had thrifted a few years ago. I was a Victorian ghost, so I had bought an old-fashioned, lace dress for four dollars. What I changed to make it the shirt you see now is that I brought the waistline up. (It used to be a drop waist.) I shortened the sleeves, changed the neckline, and made it more fitted. I also obviously made it shorter so that it could be a shirt.

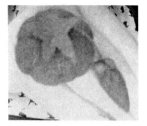

I made this ring last week. I really like it. It is supposed to look like the tomato pin cushions that people sew with.

This is a neon green walrus with a pink snout stuffed animal I made. I love his whiskers. In the instructions book, it was brown. But why settle for brown?

I really like huge scarves, but they're expensive, so I decided to make a neck cowl. I used a lot of different materials in the neck cowl. In addition to yarn I used scraps of fabric and ribbon. Another thing I used was plastic bags. I cut up and braided plastic bags and knit them into the scarf. This scarf took me forever to make but I am really happy about how it turned out. It's one of my favorite pieces. I entered it in a crafts show. I won the show for another piece I made, but I still think this one was the best. I always get lots of comments when I wear it.

Chapter 31

by Diana: The Unicorn—Part II

I was getting bored writing romance novels and women's fiction. I was a steady mid-list writer, but I wasn't having the kind of bestseller-list success that I'd dreamed about. It became hard to justify the amount of time I was putting into my work in relation to the financial reward. Life in Philadelphia was expensive, and we were going broke.

The successful writers I knew operated like small business owners. They did constant marketing, budgeting, networking, and conferencing. As more bookstores failed and on-line social media obligations proliferated (Facebook, Twitter, Goodreads, Shelfari, blogging, review websites), the ratio of writing to marketing shifted toward the latter.

The ratio of book buyers to books was also shifting alarmingly. My print runs were getting too small, and shrinking with every book. It wasn't just me; it was the business. Borders declared bankruptcy, eliminating one third of the bookstores that carried a decent fiction section. Barnes and Noble was only holding on because of the success of The Nook, their ebook reader. Fewer stores, more ebooks, more on-line marketing required to reach ereaders. It was exhausting. In 2006, I'd sell tens of thousands of books without lifting a finger. Now I was busting my butt to sell in the thousands. I had to get into the new mindset or find a different job.

I started to read business books on how to make it as an

entrepreneur. *Rich Dad, Poor Dad,* a disturbing book with a captivating message, convinced me that the only way to make real money was to never work for anyone and to build investments that would generate income. Investments, for instance, like a backlist that was all mine.

Self-publishing was exploding. Authors were keeping seventy to one hundred percent of their sales, which could be substantial due to new pricing structures like the ninety-nine cent ebook.

The math was intriguing. Why not sell an ebook for three dollars on Amazon, and take seventy percent? That was over two dollars a book. Publishers were paying authors just over eight percent for mass markets. That was less than fifty cents per book, minus fifteen percent for the agent.

It was all very confusing and confounding to watch my business change from day to day. I needed to get a new contract, but I wasn't sure I wanted one when everything was in such flux. But I also wasn't sure I wanted to become my own publisher, with all the work that entailed.

But unicorn hoodies, now there was a business that felt simple.

People were begging Hana for her product. They stopped her on the street and marveled. "I'd love one for my twin cousins! Do you have a card?"

She had commissioned quite a few hoodies by now and the number grew every time she left the house in the sweatshirt. One afternoon, she wore her hoodie to the orthodontist's office and almost caused a riot as the little girls gathered around to stare and ask questions.

But as much as the older kids liked the unicorns, I was convinced that the real market was in babies and toddlers. Plus, their product would use less fabric, be cheaper to buy, and faster to make.

Hana had more products in her arsenal. How did she make that ring? That hair band? That skirt? Could she make her friends a pair of those earrings? They were soooo coooool…

This thing could be huge.

I started to research the wholesale hoodie market.

I figured we'd start small, but have a goal.

"How do you see your future?" I asked Hana.

"I want to be Doe Deere." She paused. "And Martha Stewart, but without the jail time."

Now that was an excellent goal if I ever heard one. Two excellent role model business women for a fearless fourteen-year-old entrepreneur/artist.

Forget Harvard. We were going to shoot much higher than that.

But how does a mother help put a dream so original in motion? Sure, I could help her research the market. Drive her to the fabric store. Bankroll the first dozen hoodies.

But that stuff was the nuts and bolts, which bored me. I was more interested in the philosophy. Hana was Doe Deere. She was Martha Stewart. Her vision was insanely on-target and nuanced. How to keep that brand image pure? What was her brand image?

Good thing I'd worked in advertising.

I started to outline a business plan.

1) Shut up. When it comes to Hana, chances are, I'm wrong.

2) Listen. Her ideas are better than mine. Her worldview is fresher. She's already achieved things at fourteen that I could only dream of.

We talked and planned and schemed. I researched and talked to everyone I could find with any experience in this sort of endeavor.

I had to go to writer's conference in Connecticut the next weekend to give a workshop and do a signing. While I was there, I was thrilled to find a workshop on writing business plans given by an old friend whom I'd always admired. I took copious notes, but I wasn't thinking about my writing career; I was thinking about Hana's craft and sewing career. Books, obviously, were dead. All of us in the room knew it. But unicorn hoodies, crocheted earrings, and towering headband bows—now that was cutting edge.

I talked to my friend after the speech, and she agreed to become our business consultant. With her help, we put together a full-fledged business plan.

Within three months, we manufactured and sold three hundred hoodies, all hand-modified into splendid rainbow unicorns by Hana. We celebrated by buying our first industrial strength sewing machine to make the work go faster, because this was just the beginning. It wasn't easy sewing through all those layers of mane, and Hana had been doing parts of it by hand. Sometimes, after a long night, Hana's fingers were bloody with needle pricks. But she didn't care. The work was the thing. The work, and my help, would get her where she wanted to go. After all, it was her dream, and she was supremely talented. Wasn't it a mother's duty to develop that talent at all costs? She'd thank me later.

Doe Deere and Martha Stewart, look out!

Within three more months, her website, Hanacorn.blogspot.com, was getting 1,200 hits a day, and we couldn't keep up with the orders. We had to hire a website designer to make a platform that could handle the added volume and all the financial transactions.

We had to hire help with the sewing, too, because it was getting hard to juggle school and the work. I had started to pick her up early when I could. Who needed gym class, after all?

We hooked up with a tiny, five-person company in Old City that made handbags out of recycled seatbelts. They had a workshop on 2nd Street that they leased to us on the weekends. Hana and I and the two women we'd hired to help us sew, Louisa and Helga, would be there at six in the morning Saturday and Sunday to keep up with demand. We'd work through the day and late into the night until our hands were raw. Sometimes, Louisa would sing songs of her native Spain when the nights started feeling too long. We were exhausted all the time, but we were selling like mad and Hana was thrilled out of her mind.

Nothing to help a kid with math like calculating profits in four currencies.

Unicorn hoodies were Hana's trademark, but we were also selling rings she designed made out of tiny bows. Her headpieces with little cherries or plastic flowers were flying off the virtual shelves. Hana would design the items, then Helga, who didn't speak much English but who had done piecework in The Ukraine and knew a thing or two about production, would figure out how to make them with the least number of steps and the least waste of fabric.

It wasn't long before borrowing the handbag factory was cramping our style. We needed our own space. After selling our ten thousandth hoodie, we got it: a loft in West Philly, near enough to the University of Pennsylvania that we could enlist my husband (and even, sometimes, his grad students) if we needed extra hands or the car to ship boxes to Florida or California or even as far away as Europe and Japan.

We had a huge party to celebrate our very own factory. We bussed Hana's friends in from the suburbs on charter busses and had a great time with sushi, a chocolate fountain, and a band. Isaiah was sick as a dog from something he'd eaten earlier, or maybe just from raging jealousy and the emotional stress of having his mother disappear into his sister's life, leaving him to catch rides to his games when his father was out of town. True, I hadn't been on the soccer sidelines in ages, but soccer wasn't my thing. His dad could handle that. He understood.

In any case, I had never seen Hana smile so broadly. I had never felt so proud of my daughter. She had done this! She had worked and suffered, and achieved something beyond what most of her peers could even imagine!

The story was too good to not be noticed—local tween becomes unicorn hoodie tycoon! After only the tiniest public relations push from our new publicity firm, we got the call from our local Channel Ten, the Philadelphia NBC affiliate.

That was the link that got us on the Today *Show.*

The woman sitting next to me in the workshop coughed and I startled back to reality.

I sat up straight. I looked around me at all the people scribbling notes.

I was at a writers' conference in a Holiday Inn in North Haven, Connecticut spinning the fantasy that my child would be a hoodie magnate.

Not only that, but she'd be a happy hoodie magnate. Because, honestly, what fourteen year old who enjoys dressing up for school and impressing her friends with her sewing skills wouldn't want to give all that up to work endless hours sewing in a sweatshop?

What kind of future was I imagining for my daughter? For myself? For our family?

The workshop room was hot and crowded. I was surrounded by adults—writers and wannabe writers. They were struggling with lack of talent, or time, or resources, or knowledge. Some of them were going to make it, others were going to fall by the wayside. But they all had a dream just like I had once had a dream. To be a writer.

And I was sitting there dreaming about unicorn hoodies?

I felt ill.

I thought back to my own childhood dreams.

I had wanted to be a clown. To be the calligrapher to the Queen of England. I had wanted to be a baker. A doctor. Even an organic farmer for a while. No grown up had ever interfered with my dreams. I was able to try on ideas, one after the other, until I found the one that stuck at thirty-one years old: being a writer.

It was far-fetched.

It was a long shot.

But when I was ready (and only then), I went for it. No one forced me too early, before I was mature enough to have stories to tell. No one screamed at me and belittled me. No one interfered at all.

I looked to my friend speaking at the projector. *High Level Use Cases. Input. Output. Process. Supply. Milestones.*

I looked back down at my notes. *Where to get cheap hoodies? Where to buy cheap fleece? New sewing machine feet to get through seven mane layers? Advertising? Media training? Capital expenditures?*

I had lost my mind. I had lost it way back when, when Hana was born and I thought she rolled over the best. It was still gone, fourteen years later, as I planned her pre-teen career.

The speaker put up a Power Point slide. "The main problem," she said, "is how to get There from Here. The main question therefore is, Where is Here? Where is There?"

A bucket of cold water thrown on my head couldn't have roused me to greater attention.

Here was a writer's conference.

There was my dream—writing fiction.

My dream.

No one had ever bullied me into starting a hoodie factory.

I am here, with six published novels, because I succeeded at something my parents could never have imagined for me. I am a writer. I do something that I love because my parents butted out, let me dream. They let me change my dream over and over until I got it right—at thirty-one years old. Writers love to quote a survey from the Jenkins Group, a Michigan publishing services firm, which found that eighty-one percent of American adults want to write a book. Eight out of every ten adults believes that they have a book inside them. Even Amy Chua, the original tiger mother, admits in *Battle Hymn of the Tiger Mother* that what she really wanted to do was write "an epic novel about mother-daughter relationships." But she didn't dare try.

How ferocious was that? What the heck was that teaching her child? Forgo your true dreams and follow the shallow, predictable, status-obsessed dreams of your parents?

Why had I decided to follow my dream, when so many people hadn't? Because following my dreams was exactly what I'd always been taught to do. Being forced to slave at something chosen for you by your mother might teach you skills and hard work, but it also teaches you to give up your own dreams. No wonder tiger mothers are so angry all the time. They'd become what they never wanted to be.

Hana wanted to make twelve unicorn hoodies for her friends.

But no. Her dream had been too small for me. As soon as her dream passed her lips, I began to alter it. "Twelve hoodies? For fourteen-year-olds?" I had demanded. "Why not make them for little kids? That's where the market is."

That's where the market is? Did I even listen to myself?

Surely, I hadn't listened to her.

Hana's *Here* was my office. Sweet Hana dwarfed in my big green chair, excited and ready to go.

"Target?" I had cried. "Let's get online and see how to get them wholesale, that way, you can make more profit—"

"Okay." She'd shrugged. "But they're not for profit, they're for friends."

There for Hana was before school, at the lockers, kids milling around her. Quiet Hana, in her quiet way, handing out the hoodies, blushing slightly because they were so darn awesome. Other kids would ooh and ahh. She'd take the cash—probably not a hundred dollars, forty maybe?—and make enough for a few days of awesome thrifting. I could just imagine her and her friends traipsing through the streets of Philadelphia, Hana leading the way because she knew all the stores and knew what to look for in them. Then maybe she'd buy everyone frozen yogurt, because she could with the couple of bucks profit she still had left over.

Then she'd move on to the next thing that caught her interest.

The workshop was almost over and the speaker was taking questions. I tried to remember now how long ago Hana had asked me to take her to buy the hoodies. At least a month had passed, with her asking almost every day. Wholesale hoodies weren't as easy to research as you might imagine. Cotton or poly? Zip or no? This website or that? Buying two dozen made them cheap, but could we sell that many? Buying things over the Internet was so hard, as color and quality were hard to judge and it had to be exactly right.

That is, it had to be exactly right if you were an obsessed grown up with delusions of grandeur. If you were Hana, you'd go to Target, get what was there, and make do.

It was May. School would be over in a few weeks. Poor Hana, powerless against my delusions, had been waiting patiently. I had basically said to her, your dreams are too small. Here, let me stomp on them, toss them away, and substitute my idea of what a successful kid should look like.

I gathered my notes, went to my room, and got online to check if there was a Target I could hit on my way home the next day.

Then I made a business plan for myself, for this crazy novel-writing thing that I do, that I love, that sustains me. And I thought, *I hope that Hana finds this kind of satisfying life for herself one day.* When she does, she'll have all the skills to achieve whatever it is she wants to achieve. That is, she'll have the skill to know what she wants and to not let anyone tell her otherwise. She won't be bullied by anyone because she knows how to follow her dreams.

"What's the opposite of a Tiger?" I had asked her one day when we were brainstorming ideas for this book.

"A lemur," she said.

I was surprised.

"You know, the ones who go over the cliffs."

"A lemming?"

"Whatever. Yeah. Them. The ones who don't think, who just follow."

Tigers raise lemmings, I thought.

Humans, on the other hand, if they're very, very careful, and gentle, respectful, and aware, raise tigers.

Chapter 32

by Hana: Moving On

There was an article in the *Philadelphia Inquirer* today about how Urban Outfitters is having trouble.

I was at an Urban Outfitters last night because there was a watch I wanted online and I thought maybe I could get it at the store.

I couldn't.

But while my mom ordered it from the store (so we wouldn't have to pay shipping), I walked around, picking out stuff I liked. We weren't going to buy anything—we weren't shopping. But it was fun because when I found something I liked, I looked at the tag. Everything I liked was the same brand.

I love that I know my style so well.

I know that people think my clothes are weird. But here's the thing—a few months after I wear something, everyone else starts wearing it. I don't think that they wear my style because of me. I think that I'm just a tiny bit ahead. I like "weird" stuff, but weird just ends up meaning first when you're dealing with fashion.

So when we got home, I found the article again and reread it.

Here's what jumped out at me first: *executive creative director of product design.*

Oh. My. God. I want to do that. How do I get to do that?

Then, a few lines down: *executive director of women's apparel.*

Why don't people tell you that these jobs exist? Everyone wants you to be a lawyer or a dentist.

General merchandise manager of women's apparel for the Urban brand.

And then…wait for it…

Buying team.

I got out my notebook and started to write all this down.

"…this buying team had not been brave enough in how they were ordering merchandise and had not closely monitored what was hot among competitors and on blogs…"

This is all I do. No one would even have to pay me. They could pay me in clothes. Or accessories. Urban's accessories are amazing.

I went back and read the article two more times.

"…The hundreds of people at the Philadelphia Navy Yard in charge of selecting and buying fashions for one of the country's biggest specialty retail corporations…"

Six hundred people, and they're all in Philadelphia.

I'm in Philadelphia.

Sometimes, it feels like the world is trying to tell me something.

I have to learn about this stuff. I have to figure this all out.

I can't wait.

Chapter 33

by Diana: Battle Hymn of the Mother of a Tiger

People wonder how American parents raise such innovative, creative, kick-butt children. What is it that these parents do to create kids with the courage to follow their dreams? Kids who defy the word "stereotype"? Why are these children capable of seeing beyond the outdated, conventional (yawn!) clichés—Harvard, violin, doctor, lawyer—and into a future that most parents are too old, tradition bound, and small minded to even imagine? Well, I can tell you, because I know. Here are a few things that my children, Hana and Isaiah, are never allowed to do:

•Miss an episode of *The Office*.

•Waste their time on extracurricular activities that they don't love.

•Pass up important family or social events because they put their own personal enrichment first.

•Think that they're better than other people because of their grades. An "A" can mean *excellent*, but it also stands for *asshole*.

•Think that they're better than other people because they're ahead of them in school or extracurricular activities. Nothing is sadder than "prodigies" who end up miserable, lonely adults because everyone else catches up (and surpasses) them by adulthood.

•Brag about awards. The only achievements that matter in the end don't get awards (character, kindness, compassion, courage, friendship).

I'm using the term "American parent" loosely. Anyone who embraces the Western values of individuality, creativity, and questioning of authority can be American in my book. But let's face it, most people with these values live in America.

Quite a few of them live in my house.

The opposite of the American mother is the Chinese mother, aka, the infamous tiger mother. But I also use the term "Chinese mother" loosely. Anyone of any ethnicity can be a Chinese mother and many lovely, creative mothers I know just happen to have Asian roots. But in my East-West dictionary, "tiger mother" translates to "raging narcissist." "Discipline" means "neurosis." And "status symbol" means "child." This is why when Chinese mothers think they're being strict, Western mothers understand that they're merely being insecure, experiencing boundary issues, and really ought to see a therapist. Mostly, we see a Chinese mother's drive to force march her children to excel at the most conventional and stereotypical of pursuits as a sad attempt to try to fit in.

Western mothers say to hell with fitting in.

We want our kids to stand out.

This is why a Western mother won't encourage her child to become a grade-grubbing, rote learner. Sure, my kids get straight A's. They like schoolwork and they're good at it, so why not? It's fun and it opens doors. But I know amazing kids who get lousy grades, and my mind is open enough to see that they can be some of the most interesting, talented kids around. The day I believe that my kids' grades measure intelligence in any meaningful way is the day I throw away my Western mother badge. I refuse to fall for these narrow minded, outdated myths of success. I know that what others tell me is the best is often a marketing ploy or nostalgia for a past that no longer exists. Harvard? Maybe. But maybe not. Because the Western mother sees her child as an individual, not an emblem of her status or an extension of herself, she can entertain the idea that for many children Harvard (or violin or whatever…) is exactly the wrong choice. I have nothing against Harvard (or violins or whatever…). But these status obsessed choices can destroy a child. To see a truly gifted kid try to shoehorn herself into a mold she doesn't fit is the tragic consequence of tiger parenting.

So what is important for Western mothers if they don't value pay-to-play awards, outdated myths of success, and trumped up honors? What truly matters in the end?

Character.

That's it and it's everything and I won't apologize for it.

Are your kids good humans? If you belittle them and their desires, they'll learn to put down others and worse, to discount their own ideas. Children have to be taught compassion and respect by example. They have to be shown how to love. If a child is raised to believe that screaming insults is a form of love, then that will be how that child loves. If a child is raised to believe that what they do is more important than who they are, they will never learn unconditional love. Then, no matter how good they are, they will endure constant anxiety and stress as they try to live up to someone else's idea of who they should be.

It's ironic that when kids have character, when they are raised with respect for themselves and for others, all those worthless awards and honors come naturally. The straight A's come if they enjoy the work. The expertise and passions come if they love what they do for the thing itself, not as a means to an end. The only way to teach them this skill of loving the thing itself is to let them be children, because after all, what's more childish than having fun for the pure joy of it? Kill this impulse by stressing awards and adult-meted accolades, and you've killed any chance your child had at achieving true excellence.

Western parenting is one of the most difficult things I can think of. You have to trust someone you love to do the best thing, even if it goes against your own beliefs and desires. You have to love your children for whom they are, not for what they do or what honor they bestow upon you. I mean, upon themselves. You have to love your children, support them, and celebrate them through failure after failure, because what a parent calls failure is very likely successful (fun, magical, engaging) childhood.

Western children don't need or want a roomful of adults clapping for them. They have no desire to be dancing monkeys for anyone, especially their parents.

Western children want a roomful of adults who are horrified, confused, and awed by their audacity, originality, and fearlessness.

In a word, they want to be children.

It takes an incredibly strong mother to let that happen.

Chapter 34

by Hana: Handing Out the Hoodies

I sold twelve unicorn hoodies to kids in my class. I didn't want to make them cost a lot of money, because some kids didn't have a lot of money. But I also didn't want to lose money. Some kids asked for special prices, but how could I give a hoodie to one person for one price and give it to another person for another? It didn't feel right.

After the ninth hoodie, I broke even and I paid my mother back for the sweatshirts and the fabric.

A mother of a girl I knew suggested that I try to sell them in a store in town. They took two hoodies. It's kind of exciting.

I also did a few custom order hoodies for little kids. One was a Pegasus unicorn, with wings. That one was blue because the little girl didn't like pink.

I also started to work at little kid birthday parties doing craft projects and decorating cakes. Also face painting. It's fun and the money is nice to have. My mother said to me that I'd never have to work at a coffee shop or someplace like that because I have so many skills. But I'd like to work at a coffee shop. I think it would be fun.

Now I'm working on my Halloween costume. I always start them early because I like them to be really spectacular. I have so much fun making them perfect. I'm going to be a queen. I thrifted a great robe with some of the money I made over the summer working at the crafts camp, selling hoodies, and doing parties. I'm trying not to change the robe too much, because it's vintage and even though I got a great price on it, I know it's worth a lot.

I'm not looking forward to high school. I'm worried that it will be hard and the teachers won't be nice. They do have a great drama club, though, and everyone wants me to work on costumes.

Maybe someday, I can be the leader of the costume crew.

I hope so. If I work hard.

It's going to be a new adventure.

Chapter 35

by Diana: High School Begins with Biology

Middle school was coming to an end.

Hana came home from school one day toward the last weeks of school and said, "Did you go to the school meeting last night?"

She knew I didn't. I never went to school meetings.

"It was about high school. You have to go and find out about stuff."

"Oh. Okay. I'll call around."

"You have to do more than call around."

I was deep into my new writing project. I wanted to branch out from novels to try my hand at a non-fiction book about the crazy world of youth soccer. This was my new business plan. I had spent a lot of time looking closely at my career, and decided that I had to take more risks. That I had to be, in fact, more like Hana. Fearless.

"What are you worrying about?" I asked.

She explained. "I've gotten straight-A's every single year. So they're going to think I'm a brainiac and they're going to put me in honors classes and I'm going to fail. You have to call the right people and talk to them to make sure I'm in the regular classes."

She couldn't be right about this. Could she?

The next day, I emailed the teacher in charge of her IEP. An IEP is an Individualized Education Plan. It's a blueprint to make sure the parents and school are on the same page when your kid has a learning difference.

What was Hana's issue again? Reading? But we'd just gotten back her Pennsylvania state test scores and she'd scored at the advanced level in reading for the fourth year in a row.

Maybe it was math. But she was in grade level math now, getting A's. That couldn't be it.

Was it some orchestra thing? Not playing *Twinkle* or something? She was first chair viola in her school orchestra, so that couldn't have been it either.

Or was it all of those things, until, just like that, it wasn't?

When had she caught up to everyone else, then surpassed a good percentage of them? I tried to remember what they had told us about her learning differences. I went back to check my notes from the original meeting after all that absurd testing to find the answer. Her learning difference was that she was super smart, but failed at the specific tasks asked of her by grownups.

Maybe she hadn't changed a bit, but they'd started asking smarter questions.

Her IEP teacher emailed me right back. "Don't worry. Hana will be in all college prep courses."

I panicked. It was exactly what Hana had warned me about. I called and eventually got the teacher on the phone. "No, not college prep. Regular classes. She's worried the college prep will be too hard."

The teacher explained patiently. "College Prep means regular. Honors means advanced." She assured me I'd have this all down by Hana's senior year.

I sighed with relief. Good thing I hadn't wasted my time in a meeting.

Minutes later, the postman dropped the mail through the front door slot. A letter from the high school sat on the top of the pile. *To the parents of Hana Holquist.* These words still made my mouth go dry with dread.

Another suspension?

Another notice of a meeting I have to attend and probably won't?

It was Hana's schedule for next year. She had been placed in Honors English, Honors History and Honors Spanish.

Uh oh.

I emailed the IEP teacher again and this time copied all of Hana's other teachers on the correspondence. What was going on? We needed to fix this. Hana was going to kill me for messing up her freshman schedule. Sometimes, my hands off approach wasn't stellar.

While I waited for a reply, I got on the phone with friends who already had kids in the high school for advice on what to do now.

"I'm the only one who's going to tell you this," one mother said before launching into her complicated high school strategy, which was more like a carefully mapped out war plan, the aim of which was to get her daughters into the best college possible with the least amount of work.

"Why wouldn't anyone tell me that?" I asked when she was done outlining her truly impressive methods. I had a page and a half of scribbled notes.

"That's how competitive it is in high school. People think that by messing up your kid, theirs will get ahead."

I meant to follow through on all the information she'd given me. Or at the very least, hide Hana's schedule until I got it straightened out. But instead, I got caught up in my own work, and lost track of the day.

When the latch on the back door clicked open, I froze.

The letter from the high school was open on the kitchen counter. I was upstairs in my office.

It was too late to dash down to grab it.

I listened to Hana moving around the kitchen. Eventually, she came up the stairs and plopped into my office chair.

"Tell me things," I said, not looking up from my computer screen. "How was school?"

"I'm taking Honors English and Honors History next year," she said. "Which means that this summer, I need to take bio."

I looked up. "Honors?" *Bio?*

"Honors are the advanced classes," she explained patiently. "College Prep are the regular classes."

"I see." I tried to act casual. "A letter came from the high school with something like that. I think it's downstairs."

"I know. I saw it. Can I have the computer? I want to get on Facebook. What's for dinner?" She examined her nail polish, which as usual was exquisite. She'd given herself a French manicure except instead of white on the edge of the nail, it was scalloped pink and blue. How did she do that? It looked amazing.

"I thought you didn't want to be in honors classes," I said.

"Well, I didn't. But today, Dr. Ellis and Dr. Geckard asked me to eat lunch with them in the classroom."

"They did?"

"Yeah. Just the three of us."

"Nice."

"It was. They wanted to talk to me about high school."

"No kidding."

"They said I was too smart for college prep classes. They said that they recommended Honors History and Honors English for me. They said it didn't matter that I'm so bad at spelling because it's the ideas that count. They said a lot of those kids who spell perfectly and read fast don't have ideas. I've actually noticed that."

"So just like that, you're okay with the honors classes?"

"No. It wasn't just like that." She was fixing a non-existent mar in her polish. "I said I still thought it would be too hard. So they recommended I take bio over the summer."

I was trying to put the concepts of biology, Hana, and summer together in one image. It wasn't jelling.

"They said that bio is the hardest class in ninth grade. It'll take most of my time and energy. So if I take it over the summer, then I can concentrate on my other classes during the year."

I wanted to hunt down her teachers, throw my arms around them, and kiss them. This was exactly what the secretive mother with the battle plan had told me to get Hana to do. I had it all scribbled out on my pad. But I had dismissed the idea of a summer spent in a dingy biology classroom, sure that Hana would never consent to a summer of science.

But here she was, begging me to sign her up.

I love non-Tiger parenting.

I had her registered by the next morning.

Then, I started having second thoughts.

I was terrified that she'd be put into a class with all the kids who'd failed biology during the regular year, the ones who didn't care, who smoked pot and pierced their eyebrows. But instead, the geniuses at the high school combined the honors and college prep kids. Hana was in biology with some of the best students in the school, which would never have happened if she'd taken the class during the school year.

Every day, her carpool came at 7:20 in the morning. The other boy looked as if he'd just rolled out of bed after a hard night. But not Hana. She'd set her alarm for 6:30 a.m. and carefully dress and do her makeup and hair. She wouldn't be back home until one in the afternoon. Then she'd allow herself an hour break to eat and catch up on Facebook. When the hour was up, she'd start in on her homework. Her carpool mate, a boy who won more medals in last year's Science Olympiad than anyone else in the middle school told us that he usually finished all his homework during the snack break.

It would take Hana two hours to get through it.

Then she'd break for a quick dinner. While the rest of us lingered around the table, talking and catching up, she'd excuse herself and go back to studying until she was too exhausted to keep her eyes open.

She did this for four weeks.

"It doesn't matter if you get an A or not," I'd remind her. She was getting an A, but it was killing her. "Nothing wrong with a B. This is science. Not everyone is good at it. I know I'm not." She'd been asking me for help, but I didn't have a clue about biology. I'd call my brother the physicist on the phone and he'd send long emails detailing how to figure out the probability of tall, green pea plants or short yellow ones, or how to calculate the focal length of an electron microscope. I'd forward them to Hana.

"I want to prove that I can do this," she'd say.

"Prove what? To whom? It doesn't matter," I'd assure her.

"For myself. I know I can do it."

By the fifth week, she was totally burnt out. I thought, *this is where it will all fall apart.*

Instead, she'd set her alarm for five-thirty in the morning. She'd get dressed, eat, feed the cats, then start in on the studying that she was too tired to do the night before.

She'd tell me stories about kids' parents coming in to talk to the teacher.

"Joe's dad wanted to know if there was anything he could do to catch up. Like extra credit or something."

"He's not a good student?"

"He's a total brainiac. He just doesn't do the work."

"What did the teacher say?"

"The teacher said no. They got in a big fight."

"Poor Joe," I said. *Poor teacher.*

"Poor Joe?" She rolled her eyes. "He should have turned in the homework. The smart kids might be smart at some stuff, but they're really dumb at other stuff. Why not just do the homework if it's so easy for them?"

I ran into another mother at the grocery store who had a girl in the class. She rolled her eyes and moaned. "We had to make a schedule that her therapist made her sign," the mother told me. "The deal is, no TV or video games or going out with her friends until she's done the homework. But I don't think I can keep up six weeks of policing this and the nanny is no help at all. I wish we'd never signed her up for summer school. If she gets a B—" The mother trailed off, unable to express the dire consequences of such an awful tragedy.

I couldn't quite get my head around this babying of fourteen-year-old kids. If they didn't want to be there, why did they go? If they didn't do the work, why not let them suffer the consequences?

But I knew the answer. The parents had pushed them to get ahead. My kid was there on her own accord, willing to do whatever it took so that she could take Honors English and Honors History. I couldn't have been prouder of her. But I'd never say this to the mother. I just nodded in sympathy. "Yeah, it's a lot of work."

By now I fully understood that the work was to butt the heck out so the child could take ownership of her own destiny. But this was too hard to explain in the check-out aisle.

Hana was almost always the last one to emerge from the school. Her carpool buddy Sam and I would sit in the car, watching the students stream out of the building. Eventually, the buses would leave. I'd ask Sam questions about the Science Olympiad, a truly astonishing event. He chose an area of study—maybe astronomy or earth science—and studied it in depth for months. Then he competed in that area against teams from all over the region. When he won—and he usually did—he'd go to Nationals. Sam's face would light up as he told me the stories. Like Isaiah on the soccer field, or Hana in the mall, he'd found his true love. I loved this kid.

Finally, Hana would emerge from the building.

"Sorry, I didn't know how to make a graph in Excel."

Good that she stayed and asked, because I didn't know how to do it either.

The second-to-last day of the sixth week was the final. Meiosis, mitosis, photosynthesis, carbon cycles, cell cycles, respiration, fermentation, and mitochondria. There was math. There were chemical formulas. Her stack of homemade flashcards was five inches high.

She studied until she couldn't keep her eyes opened. Then she woke up early, and studied some more.

I was sick with worry.

On the last day, we got the news: she'd earned her very first high

school A.
     Not that I cared.
     But she did.
     She cared a lot.
     Which was, when you come to think of it, pretty darn cool.

Chapter 36

by Hana: I Love Asians

I was afraid that my Asian friends would be mad since I was working on this book, so I just wanted to put that out there: I love you guys.

Some people say that's racist, but I don't think it is. I think it's a compliment.

I especially love Kevin Wu. He's the stereotypical Asian: short, wears glasses, plays violin, is super-smart, and really good at science. When he walks down the hall with his friend Jack (also Asian), they look like father and son. It's really cute. Kevin hates China. You want to get him going, tell him that you think China is awesome. He'll ask you if you know what communism is. I don't really know what it is, but I pretend to like it just to make him mad.

Jack is a rebel Asian. He plays the flute.

Kyle Tong is also a rebel Asian—he's not taking honors bio this summer. This is why we call him by his gangster name, K-Tong.

Henry Wu and Jamie Lin say that their parents would kill them if they got anything wrong on a test, but it never happens, so how would they know? In fact, I think it's the one thing they don't know. (Try it, guys! Venture into the unknown!)

Once, our teacher gave us a reading assignment on the meatpacking industry. Everyone went on Facebook whining. *Ew, we can't do it. It's too gross! My mom is calling the teacher.* The Asians were like, grow up and just do it. They can't get out of it. Their parents won't side with them.

Asians make the rest of us look like whiners.

I took biology in summer school after eighth grade to get it out of the way, but I was terrified. I suck at science, and my parents are just as hopeless.

"See if you can find someone to tutor you," my mom said. "Do you know any of the other kids?"

"Yeah, just about every single Asian in my class is taking bio over the summer." They want to get it out of the way so they can take two math classes freshman year or something like that.

If I take it, I can have an easier schedule and have time to be in orchestra.

"So, do you like any of these kids? Can you hire one?"

The Asians I like have tea in the morning before school with the orchestra teacher. *I know.* You can't make this stuff up.

So I went and asked if any of them could tutor me over the summer. "And tell me how much you charge."

"Oh, Hana," Louis said. "We help everyone all the time. You don't have to pay us. Just ask."

See. Don't you love those guys?

But I brought Louis and Kevin homemade chocolate chip cookies the next day. I think they thought I was nuts, but they don't know how bad I am at science.

I didn't know either, come to think of it, because I aced the class. They helped me sometimes, but mostly I did it myself.

Chapter 37

by Diana: The Finish Line

I told Hana that the first draft of this book was finally finished. We were at a coffee shop, waiting for Isaiah to finish his soccer practice. She was doing her homework. I was formatting the last chapters.

"I don't get it," Hana said. "I'm only into my first semester of high school. How can we write a book saying that I'm a success?"

"We can't," I agreed. "But think about it, at what point can anyone say a person is a success? After a year of high school? After getting into college? After a first job?"

"That's a good place," she said. "The first job."

"But why there? That's just as random as the first semester of high school. So many things can go wrong after the first job. Maybe that first job leads you to a fantastic, lucrative career. After twenty excellent years, they throw you a big party. Then you go home and throw yourself on your bed, weeping, because finally you admit to yourself that you've wasted your entire life. All you ever wanted was to be a belly dancer, and now it's too late."

She stared at me. "I have to get this math homework done."

"All I'm saying is, you can't judge from the surface at some random point in life who's a success and who's not. You can't pick a moment and say, 'That's it. That's the proof right there. I was right.'"

She mulled this over. She looked a little disappointed.

"It's sort of the point of this whole book, really," I said, trying to cheer her up. "That life is constantly changing. It isn't one straight-forward trajectory. It's got ups and downs. At least, an examined life has ups and downs. The real tragedy, the only failure, is when a person lives an unexamined life. When they do what they do because someone told them to or because they want to please someone or they care what someone else thinks. Before they know it, they don't know any other way to be." I told her how many people I ran into who tell me that they want to write books. I explained that I always said, "Go for it!" But the people never did. "That's the only real failure. And it can happen when you're in high school or in a great job or at a great school."

She looked up. "I stopped listening to you a while back. I really have to get this math homework done."

"Are you even going to read the book?"

"I guess I should."

"Maybe you shouldn't."

This seemed to please her. She was awfully busy.

"It's my narrative of your life. Maybe you shouldn't be burdened with what I say, how I organize things."

"But it'll be out in the world."

"Sure. And everyone will read something different into it. Just like you will. Believe me, I've written enough books to know that no matter what you write, everyone thinks that you're writing about them."

We sipped our chai for a while. She went back to her math problems.

"I have to give it to my first readers this Friday," I said.

"Do it."

So I did.

A few weeks later, I got the manuscripts back.

On a whim, I had sent a copy to my father-in-law and his wife. She was a wildly successful analyst and an amazing business woman. I had never met anyone quite like her. To my surprise, she insisted that she had to speak to me.

She got me on the phone. "The problem with the book is that you aren't ambitious," she told me.

I'm not sure what to make of this, but I didn't like it.

"Amy Chua didn't tell the truth in her Tiger Mother book," my mother-in-law said. "She told one truth. You have to do that. Tell a stronger story. The manuscript the way it is makes you sound weak. If you want to sell a lot of books, you have to sound powerful and strong. You are, I hate to tell you, a bit pathetic in this version."

I considered this advice.

Then forgot it.

I didn't want to sound strong. I wanted parents to know that every choice I made was agonizing. I wanted readers to feel my pain, because parenting was and is a constant struggle, fraught with difficulties. I didn't want to pretend to be an expert. I wanted to tell a personal story of one child and one mother. My joy was in the writing of this book. I didn't care how many books we sold, which I suppose made my mother-in-law right about my lack of ambition.

That was okay.

Hana had enough ambition for the two of us combined.

Chapter 38

by Hana: Write Your Own Book

What? Is the book over? Good, I was getting tired of it.

I've got to go; I have a lot of things to do, and this is taking up way too much of my time and my mother's time.

Good luck with everything.

Be yourself. Don't be afraid to tell your parents that they're old and unfashionable and that they don't really understand the world anymore.

Don't be afraid to change your mind. Often.

Don't spend too long reading other people's books.

Write your own.

Why not?

Don't you have something to say?

Acknowledgments

This book would not be possible without the insane bravery of both of my kids, who were willing to expose themselves, warts and all, for your scrutiny. I admire them for knowing that being perfect is not only impossible, but it's not what it's cracked up to be.

Also, a huge shout out to my beta readers, Ellen Hartman, Carolyn Pouncy, Peter Kaplan, Michael Holquist and Elise Snyder. Your collective wisdom and good grammar were invaluable.

A huge thank you to Chris Flores, the amazing Haverford College student who shot and designed the cover.

I wanted to add a word here, also, for my dear husband. We left him out of this book, even though he's the bedrock on which we all stand. He's a huge part of our family, and leaving him out of this book was his choice. He claims that he will, however, take part if they make a reality TV version of our lives.

I'd also like to say a word about how this book was written.

A year ago, I had started to do research for a book I'm writing about soccer mothers. After every soccer game, I'd interview as many people as were willing to speak to me. Soon, the conversations after the games became almost as important to us as the games themselves. I would take notes, then type them up, keeping them as close to the actual words and trying to maintain the distinct voice of the speaker.

These turned into surprisingly wonderful essays.

So when we decided to write this book, I knew that we'd do it the same way. I'd interview Hana about her life, and when she felt like it, she'd talk. I'd take notes, then transcribe them into her chapters. Some chapters came together fully in twenty minutes. Others, over the course of many conversations, took many months. Still others I would find when I returned from making dinner or talking on the phone—Hana had typed them when the inspiration struck. I'd go back and correct the spelling and grammar.

In this way, we put together everything we thought was important about our lives.

Hope you enjoy reading it as much as we enjoyed writing it.

Please visit http://TIGERDAUGHTER.com or http://dianaholquist.com to stay in the dialogue.

Or, if you're under twenty, you might enjoy http://Hanacorn.blogspot.com more because I have no part in that. It's all Hana all the time.

Just the way it ought to be.

CPSIA information can be obtained at www.ICGtesting.com
Printed in the USA
LVOW102215190812

295014LV00008B/139/P